ON THE SHELF

REVISITING REJECTED AND
ABANDONED SCRIPTS

ON THE SHELF

REVISITING REJECTED AND ABANDONED SCRIPTS

THEBES PUBLISHING

CONTENTS

Iain McLaughlin

FOREWORD
BY JULIANNE TODD

Iain didn't want to do this book. He wasn't interested in going back to look at projects he had locked away at the back of his head. Actually what his email said was 'who's going to give a stuff about failures?'. (Actually, I edited that – he didn't say 'stuff'.) The fact that you are holding this book suggests that someone is interested in these stories. Personally, I am fascinated by writers and *how* they write. As someone who only just had her first novel published I am also interested in how a writer would look at their earlier work, and what he would do to alter it. Iain is always very critical of his own writing. Back in the 1980s we used to look at comics he had written, and he would bemoan that he had missed the chance for a gag. In 2001 I congratulated him on *The Eye of the Scorpion*, his first *Doctor Who* story for Big Finish. His first reaction was to say he'd screwed up a line of dialogue for Peri in episode 3. He complained about how easy it would have been to fix, just by giving the Doctor a line of dialogue in reply. That always stuck with me. For years now I have been nagging him to go public with some of his stories that didn't go anywhere, to share them with people and to critique them to see what he thinks is wrong with them, and what he would do differently with the stories now. I've finally been able to pin him down and get him to do this. I enjoyed his scripts and his proposals, and I do wish some had been produced. However, the real gold for me comes in his essays on the stories, which gives a real insight into his thinking processes during the writing and also some incredibly useful advice to anyone who has an interest in writing.

Iain McLaughlin

Rejection

Introduction by Iain McLaughlin

I read a very interesting thing recently on the BBC's *Writer's Room* website. Paul Abbott, one of the best dramatists in the UK, said something like 'writing is rewriting'. He's right. A huge part of being a writer is rewriting. Often it's about rewriting what you think is really good work, and occasionally you have to rewrite something you think is really good into something you think isn't as good, because that's what you're asked to do by a producer or script editor.

Writing is often something else, too. Writing is very often about rejection.

If you have ever written, then I'm damn sure that at some point you've been rejected. I'm pretty certain that some of the work you've had rejected was really very good. At least you think it was really good. And you *should* think that. If you send work to a producer thinking it's crap you're in trouble. However, even though you think your script is a winner, there's a better than even chance that it's going to wind up landing back on your doormat or pinging into your Inbox.

That is a horrible moment. The thud of a script hitting the mat is incredibly depressing. All your work, sent back unwanted. It feels like you've wasted your time, and sometimes it makes you wonder if you haven't been wasting your time on a career you're not actually suited for. Sometimes it even makes you wonder if you're in the right job. Can you actually write at all? You know something? If you feel that way, you are not alone. Everybody who has ever written has felt that way. I've spoken to lots of writers and we've swapped stories of rejection. In a strange way, our rejections have become badges of honour. We wrote, we were rejected, we kept writing, we got more rejections, we kept writing and

3

ultimately we got commissions. These rejections are really important. They serve a lot of useful purposes. They make a writer go back and look at their work, and makes them analyse their writing to see what it was that didn't hit the spot. If they're lucky there will have been feedback about the script or story, and that can all be used as a hugely important learning experience. Rejections can really hurt but they don't have to be completely negative experiences.

It's also worth remembering this: the people who accept your work or reject it are human beings. They make professional judgements but a lot of the time, those judgements come down to a gut feeling or personal taste. Sometimes they are also affected by the fact that somebody just had a crummy day or had an argument with their partner that morning. Sometimes professionals just get it wrong. I once contacted an agent looking for representation. He replied that I shouldn't try to write, that I didn't have any talent. A week later *The Eye of the Scorpion* was commissioned. I've now written more than a dozen novels, a dozen more short stories, more than forty radio or audio plays and I've written for TV. I've had professional commissions to write *James Bond*, *Doctor Who*, *Blake's 7* and *Sherlock Holmes* as well as a healthy list of original projects. Sometimes the people deciding *yea* or *nay* get it wrong. But when they do get it wrong... *you* still have to deal with that rejection letter. It's worth remembering though, the Beatles, the Rolling Stones and J.K Rowling all got multiple rejections before they got contracts.

The other really thing about getting a rejection is that it forces a writer to develop a thicker skin and that is something every writer is going to need. You are going to get rejected from time to time. In fact, you're going to get rejected regularly. There are far more writers than there are opportunities for writers, so you have to fight for them. Sometimes you're going to lose out. Developing a thicker hide will make that easier to deal with, though the truth is, getting turned down is never pleasant.

Reproduced in this book are some stories I've pitched and submitted over the years. We're going to reproduce the pitches in full and then tell you why they were rejected, if that information was supplied. If I didn't get that feedback, I'll take a look at the story and tell you why I think it may have been rejected. I'll also tell you how I would work on the story now to make it work better.

If you find some of these stories interesting, I'll be delighted, but I hope you'll find the analysis and observations of the work useful and informative. Personally, I have always been fascinated to discuss the writing process with other writers. I'm intrigued by their techniques and, I think, one of the most important things a writer can do is constantly learn about the craft – learn from other writers, learn from your own mistakes.

And whatever you do... enjoy writing.

Iain McLaughlin

The Point of No Return

A one hour drama written for American radio drama broadcasters.

ON THE SHELF

SCENE 1. INT. ENDEAVOUR INFIRMARY.
IT SOUNDS METALLIC. CAPTAIN WILLIAM BLAKE, A
PRECISE SAILING MAN IS JOINED BY HIS XO, JOHN
FLETCHER. A COLD ATMOSPHERE.

FLETCHER: Captain. The Doctor asked me to come. He has
             the results.

BLAKE: Obviously.
             (BEAT)
             It's not comfortable, is it, John? Being alone with
             someone you've betrayed. Someone who called
             you a friend.

FLETCHER: I'd still be your friend if you hadn't pushed the
             crew so far.

BLAKE: Your manner of friend I can well live without, Mr
             Fletcher. If I am found unfit for command, my
             career is over. You will have ruined thirty years
             of dedication and hard work.

FLETCHER: I won't take responsibility for that. The blame lies
             with no-one but yourself. You forced me into this.
             You're obsessed.

BLAKE: No. I simply do my duty. But you say I am
             obsessed.

FLETCHER: You've always been driven but in the past few
             months you've gone past that. I've watched it
             happen.

BLAKE: And done nothing. Yes. You have watched a
             great many things happen and done nothing about
             them, Mr Fletcher.

FLETCHER: Maybe I should have done something sooner, but
             you were my friend.

9

BLAKE: Then tell me – friend – when did my great
            obsession begin?

FLETCHER: Probably even before you promoted me.

BLAKE: A mistake I will admit to.

FLETCHER: Your actions after we lost Mr Stewart should have
            alerted me.

BLAKE: My actions indeed? A captain's actions.

FLETCHER: Perhaps...

BLAKE: I led my men onto that shuttle. A captain would
            do no less.

FLETCHER: Should a captain have left his men on that planet
            while the ship went off surveying another world?

DIALOGUE FADES INTO FLASHBACK SCENES.

BLAKE: Regulations were followed and I was on the flight
            deck when we were due to rendezvous.

SCENE 2. ENDEAVOUR FLIGHT DECK.
SHIP OPERATING – SOUNDS LIKE A SUBMARINE RATHER
THAN THE SPACESHIP IT IS.

BLAKE: (VOICE ECHOES A LITTLE ON SPEAKERS)
            All hands, this is the Captain. Stand by to drop
            out of light speed.

FLETCHER: Fifteen seconds. Ten.

BLAKE: Mr Vasquez, bring us under light speed.

FLETCHER: I hate this.

BLAKE: (QUIETLY)
            Nervous, John?

FLETCHER: I know the inertial systems keep us on an even keel but going from faster than light to a few thousand kilometres per hour in a couple of seconds? I always worry I'm going to get splattered on a bulkhead.

MILLER: There's nothing to worry about. The mechanics of warping space means that the ship doesn't really move at all. The space around it does.

BLAKE: You're a scientist, Mr Miller. John is like myself, of the old school, a sailor. Your computers are fine and well, but even out here, we could navigate by the stars alone.

MILLER: Why would you want to, though ?

BLAKE: The Lord save us from the young. Hail the shuttle.

FLETCHER: Hailing. Aye, sir. No response. Their communications system could be damaged. She's not making any move to enter the hangar bay either. We could bring her in by remote.

BLAKE: Yes, that's possible communications are out I suppose, but it's still peculiar, I say. Bring her in and have Doctor Flower meet us in the hangar.

SCENE 3. SHUTTLE. INT.
THE SHUTTLE SOUNDS DEAD. JUST A WET, DRIPPING SOUNDS. THEN THE SOUND OF THE HATCH BEING OPENED. VOICES SOUND MUFFLED WHEN THEY SPEAK – THEY'RE ALL WEARING ATMOSPHERE SUITS. SOUNDS OF THE BREATHING APPARATUS ON THE SUITS. FOOTSTEPS IN THE SHIP.

BLAKE: Stewart? It's Captain Blake.

FLETCHER: O'Leary, check the power unit.

O'LEARY: Right, Sir.

FOOTSTEPS HEAD AWAY.

FLETCHER: Something's not right here. Mr Stewart should
              have come out of here long ago. Where are they?

BLAKE: Up here. What's left of them anyway.

FX: FOOTSTEPS MOVE FORWARD.

FLETCHER: Dead?

BLAKE: See for yourself. Doctor Flower, if you please.

FLETCHER: That stuff on their skin – it's like a kind of
              fungus. It's coming away in my hand – the skin
              with it.

BLAKE: Don't touch it, John. Not until the doctor has done
              his analysis.

FX: FOOTSTEPS APPROACH.

FLETCHER: Doctor.

FLOWER: The other five are back there. All dead. The same
              as this. It looks like they became infected by a
              fungus of some sort. I can't be sure until I've
              done a complete set of tests.

BLAKE: I want the bodies examined straight away. But do
              it here. I don't want to risk that... whatever it is
              getting onto the Endeavour. Mr Fletcher, go over
              the ship. Find all their notes and records. We still
              need to know about that planet.

SCENE 5. CAPTAIN'S CABIN INT.
SOOTHING MUSIC PLAYS. A KNOCK AT THE DOOR.

BLAKE: Come.

FX: DOOR OPENS. FLETCHER ENTERS.

BLAKE: John. Those are Mr Stewart's reports, I assume. I hope they make better reading than Dr Flower's post mortems.

FLETCHER I wouldn't bet my pension on it, Captain.

BLAKE: Damn it, that planet looked ideal for colonisation. Ideal. The gravity was perfect, the temperature just what we need and it was flourishing with plant life.

FLETCHER: Apparently all of it toxic to humans. Even the air's deadly. It's filled with microbes that after a few days...

BLAKE: ... leave you like Stewart and the others. The doctor's reports said as much. Sit down, John. You're closer to the men than I am. How have they taken these deaths?

FLETCHER: They all know the dangers involved in deep space exploration. It's more the manner of these deaths that has them on edge. They'll start getting back to normal after the funerals. I've scheduled them for tomorrow morning. Ten hundred. I know it's quick, but I thought it best to get it over with.

BLAKE: Wise, but bring them forward to tonight. There's another planet in this system that needs surveying. Work's the best thing for a crew that's had a loss like this. You don't agree?

FLETCHER: Wouldn't it be better to give them a chance to come to terms with the loss of their friends?

BLAKE: No. Best to keep their minds occupied with work. They'll grieve in their own good time. It sounds harsh, I know, but it's for the best. Any other business?

13

FLETCHER: Only more bad news. The microbe that killed the
              shuttle party – it doesn't just attack living matter.
              It eats its way through metal, plastic – even the
              padding in the shuttle's chairs is being eaten
              away. We estimate all of it will be affected within
              two days. The only positive is that it hasn't spread
              to Endeavour yet. Since the doctor can't offer us
              any protection against this microbe, we see only
              one option. Jettison the shuttle. But this thing's
              already taken half a dozen of our crew. I resent
              losing the shuttle to it as well.

BLAKE: There's no malice in nature, John. The microbe is
              only doing what is has to in order to survive. We
              must do the same and jettison the shuttle.

FLETCHER: I know it makes sense – but I still don't like it.

BLAKE: That's why I picked you for this voyage, John.
              You don't like losing. It's also the reason I'm
              promoting you to acting first officer to replace Mr
              Stewart. Technically Doctor Flower does outrank
              you, but apart from being needed where he is, he
              has no command training. I've already informed
              him and he agrees with my decision.

FLETCHER: Then, thank you. I'll go and see to the shuttle.

BLAKE: Carry on.

SCENE 6: ENDEAVOUR INT.
SOMBRE, FUNEREAL MUSIC PLAYS.

BLAKE: We are gathered here to say a farewell to our
              friends and shipmates. Though we feel their loss
              keenly, we can take a measure of comfort from
              knowing that they died performing their duty.
              Each of us knows when we sign aboard a deep
              exploration mission that there is danger. It is how
              we deal with that danger that defines who and
              what we are. Our shipmates saw the chance to

> explore this new world not as something to be
> feared, but as an opportunity to aid their fellow
> man. The planet they explored proved unsuitable
> for colonisation, their sacrifice is not a vain one.
> Future Earth ships will know not to set foot on
> that world because of our crewmates. And so we
> commend their bodies to the same space they
> gave their lives exploring. Mr Fletcher.

FLETCHER: Outer hatch open.

BLAKE: Ashes to ashes, dust to dust. We are made of
starstuff and to the stars we must all eventually
return.

FX: SOUND OF COFFINS BEING EJECTED.

FLETCHER: Coffins ejected. Closing outer hatch. Crew,
dismissed.

FX: SOUNDS OF CREW FILING OUT.

BLAKE: Get us under way for the fourth planet in this
system.

FLETCHER: Aye, sir.

BLAKE: Perhaps our luck will change tomorrow.

FLETCHER: I hope so.

VASQUEZ: (passing)
It can't get any worse.

BLAKE: What was that, Mr Vasquez? I didn't hear you.

VASQUEZ: Nothing, Sir.

BLAKE: Good. You have the flight deck, Mr Fletcher. I'll
be in my quarters if you need me.

FX: BLAKE DEPARTS.

FLETCHER: A hint, Vasquez. Insulting your captain is not a good career move.

VASQUEZ: I was only agreeing with him.

FLETCHER: Back to the flight deck. And steady as she goes.

SCENE 7. INFIRMARY. PRESENT.
BLAKE AND FLETCHER TOGETHER.

BLAKE: I should have known on that day, that you would let me down, John.

FLETCHER: How? I'd just supported you when one of the crew spoke out of turn.

BLAKE: Oh, that is a nothing. No, you allowed the wake for the dead crewmen. And you attended it yourself.

FLETCHER: What's wrong with that?

BLAKE: Everything, Mr Fletcher. Everything.

SCENE 8: INT. ENDEAVOUR MESS HALL.
SOUNDS OF A WAKE.

VASQUEZ: Y'know Doc, Taylor might have been a pain in the bum but I'm going to miss the lazy toad. He owed me fifty credits from last week's card game.

FLOWER: He owed everybody fifty credits from last week's card game. This is the first dry wake I ever been to. Still, regulations say no alcohol on board ship.

FX: SOUNDS OF DRINKS BEING POURED.

O'LEARY: Have I ever let you down, lads?

VASQUEZ: O'Leary, you're a genius.

O'LEARY: Well, I have to do something to keep busy down
              in that engine room all day. Just don't let on to the
              officers, not even Fletcher.

FLOWER: I am an officer, O'Leary. Sort of.

FX: DOOR OPENS. SUDDEN SILENCE.

FLOWER: Captain Blake.

BLAKE: What's going on here ?

O'LEARY: It's a sort of a wake, sir.

BLAKE: A wake, is it? Who organised this? You, Mr
              O'Leary?

O'LEARY: Yes, sir.

FLETCHER: I gave him permission, captain.

BLAKE: You did, Mr Fletcher. Well then, carry on.

FX: WAKE CONTINUES IN A MORE MUTED FASHION.

BLAKE: A word, Mr Fletcher.

FX: FOOTSTEPS MOVE ASIDE A LITTLE.

BLAKE: Well?

FLETCHER: I thought it would do the lads good to let off some
              steam, Captain. It's only off-duty personnel that
              are here. Everybody else is at their posts.

BLAKE: You didn't think I should be consulted about this?

FLETCHER: I didn't think it was worth bothering you to be
              honest. It's just a little morale booster, that's all.

17

BLAKE: Probably not a bad idea, either. Very well, but in future, keep me informed of these sort of things. A captain should know what's going on aboard his own ship.

FLETCHER: Yes, captain.

BLAKE: And see to it that this is finished by 22.30. We all have a long day tomorrow. 22.30, Mr Fletcher, no later.

FX: BLAKE'S FOOTSTEPS HEAD OUT.

O'LEARY: What was that?

FLETCHER: You heard the Captain. 22.30.

SCENE 9: INFIRMARY. PRESENT.
FLETCHER AND BLAKE.

BLAKE: Had you started planning to betray me even then, I wonder?

FLETCHER: You're being absurd, William.

BLAKE: Captain! You will address me as captain. I am still captain am I not?

FLETCHER: As you wish, captain.

BLAKE: I heard the crew's reaction to my order that the wake finish by 22.30. A first officer worth his salt would have put them in their place but not you. I heard you laugh with them.

FLETCHER: We weren't laughing about that.

BLAKE: I do not believe a word you say, sir.

FLETCHER: I was right – you were turning paranoid even then. Is that the reason you insisted on leading the mission down to the next planet? It is, isn't it? You thought I was trying to win over the crew so you took charge.

BLAKE: I showed leadership.

FLETCHER: Your leadership got another crewman killed.

BLAKE: I will not take blame for that. The planet was a honeycomb of tunnels. The surface was as brittle as an egg-shell. Lee fell through. There was nothing we could do for him. We were lucky to get O'Leary out of there before he fell as well.

FLETCHER: Lee fell into an underground river. You could have tracked it and found him.

BLAKE: He fell forty metres at least, and Mr Lee could not swim. Nor did we have any way of tracking the path of the river.

FLETCHER: You didn't try to find a way. You just abandoned him.

BLAKE: I could not save Mr Lee but I could save the rest of my landing crew. I would not risk their lives.

FLETCHER: Did you think to ask whether they would want to risk their lives for their friend?

BLAKE: This is a ship, Mr Fletcher, not a democracy.

FLETCHER: It shouldn't be a dictatorship.

BLAKE: Dictatorship, is it?

FLETCHER: Yes. And not a benign one. It showed when you got back from that planet.

SCENE 10. ENDEAVOUR INT.

COMPUTER: Hangar deck repressuriosed.

FX: CLANG OF HATCH. BLAKE COMES THROUGH.

FLETCHER: Captain.

BLAKE: Mr Fletcher, dismiss the crew and prepare a funeral service for Mr Lee. This time, no wake. And have Mr Miller set a course for the Capella star system.

FLETCHER: Now, sir?

BLAKE: Yes, sir. Now. Unless you have a good reason for a delay.

FLETCHER: We've lost seven crewmembers in this system. That leaves us short of manpower. The men will expect us to turn back – to pick up extra crew if nothing else.

BLAKE: And what do you think?

FLETCHER: With their morale so low, I don't think it's a bad idea.

BLAKE: Then we shall work this lack of morale out of them. They'll all have to take extra duty shifts to cover for the men we have lost. We'll sweat it out of them. Sweat it out, I say. And we are due to receive messages from home tomorrow. That should raise their spirits. And Mr Fletcher.

FLETCHER: Captain?

BLAKE: I should prefer it if you stopped questioning my orders. I am captain of this ship. Remember that.

FLETCHER: Yes, captain.

SCENE 11. ENDEAVOUR INT.
CREW LUGGING GEAR.

MILLER: Light speed in ten minutes. All hands make ready.

O'LEARY: I don't believe it.

FX: FOOTSTEPS.

O'LEARY: Mr Fletcher. He's not serious about carrying on, is he?

FLETCHER (SNAPPING – VERY SHARP)
Just get on with your duty, O'Leary.

O'LEARY: Aye, sir.

FLETCHER (A BIT GUILTY)
O'Leary. You and Croftie get yourselves checked over by the M.O. before you go back on duty.

O'LEARY: Yes, sir.

SCENE 12: ENDEAVOUR FLIGHT DECK.
THE ENGINES THROB, THE SHIP IS OPERATING
EFFICIENTLY.

VASQUEZ: Warp bubble intact. Light speed... now. Light plus point one... plus point two.

BLAKE: Light Speed 4 and hold us steady, Mr Vasquez. Time to Capella system at this velocity?

MILLER: Thirty five days, eight hours, approximately.

BLAKE: Excellent, Mr Miller. What do you say? Excellent.

SCENE 13. INFIRMARY. INT. PRESENT.
BLAKE AND FLETCHER.

FLETCHER: You didn't care what the crew thought, did you?

BLAKE: It wasn't my place to care for the crew. It was their place to follow orders.

FLETCHER: And they did.

BLAKE: Indeed?

FLETCHER: Yes. Most of them.

BLAKE: But you would defend them. You would have them follow you. You have defended and protected them, haven't you?
(NO ANSWER)
Haven't you?

SCENE 14. MESS HALL.
SOUNDS OF EATING AND ARGUING.

O'LEARY: What do you call this, Pots ?

POTS: If I told you, O'Leary, you wouldn't eat it.

O'LEARY: I'm tempted not to eat it anyway.

FX: DOOR OPENS.

FLETCHER: Listen up, everybody. I'm sorry to interrupt your breakfast. Although you should probably thank me for it…

POTS: Cheek. You could eat your breakfast off the floors in my kitchens.

FLETCHER: As I was saying, I'm sorry to interrupt, but you've got messages from home.

FX: EXCITEMENT. FOOD ABANDONED.

POTS: Why does he always do this at breakfast ?

O'LEARY: Because he likes us.

FLETCHER: Chong... Fox... O'Leary... Take your time, boys. Everybody's got a message disc.

O'LEARY: Brilliant. Who are you expecting to hear from, Vasquez?

VASQUEZ: Not sure. There was a girl I knew in New Tokyo.

O'LEARY: I didn't know you were romancing a moon-maid.

VASQUEZ: And the reason you haven't romanced one is that they hate being called moon-maids. And we're engaged.

O'LEARY: Who needed to go all the way to the moon when there was a fine lass in my own part of town? Lovely Lara. I'll be off to my bunk to see what she has to say.

SCENE 15: CAPTAIN'S CABIN.
COMPUTER BLIPS AND CHIRPS.

BLAKE: Computer, display message from Mary Blake.
(BEGINS READING)
... the children have messages for you. They keep asking when you're coming home. They miss you, William. I do, too. I wish you could come home now.
(SOFTLY)
So do I, Mary.
(RESUMES READING)
Things are getting worse here every day. There have been riots on the lunar colonies and on Mars. There are too many people and not food and air for them all. I hope you can find us a new planet soon, William. God knows, we need one.
(THOUGHTFULLY – AN EMOTIONAL MOMENT OF TRUE HUMANITY.)
I will. I promise I won't let you down. I can't.

SCENE 16: O'LEARY'S BUNK. EXT.
SOBBING FROM INSIDE.

VASQUEZ: O'Leary? O'Leary, are you all right? What is it?
             Talk to us, O'Leary. O'Leary?

NO REPLY. ONLY MORE SOBBING.

SCENE 17: MESS HALL.
FLETCHER ADRESSING THE CREW.

FLETCHER: Okay, listen up. We're going to have to run a new
             work schedule to cover the men we've lost. It
             breaks down to an extra hour each every other
             day…

O'LEARY: (SLURRED AND DRUNK)
             What are they doing out here ?

FLETCHER: Same as us, O'Leary. Earning a living.

O'LEARY: What are we doing out here? We shouldn't be
             here. We belong on a planet not in metal boxes
             floating in space.

FLETCHER: What's the matter with you, O'Leary? You're
             drunk.

O'LEARY: What can I say?

FLETCHER: You're off duty. Go to your bunk and sleep it off.

O'LEARY: Who died and made you God ? Oh, I forgot. It
             was Mr Stewart.

FLETCHER: Get him out of here.

FX: O'LEARY DRAGGED AWAY.

O'LEARY: Get off. Get your hands off me.

VASQUEZ: (QUIETLY)
              He's taking Lee's death badly.

FLETCHER: We all are, Vasquez.

VASQUEZ: You weren't down that hole with him when he
              fell. We were. There's something else. When the
              messages came in – his girlfriend dumped him.
              They'd been together eight years.

FLETCHER: Put him in the brig.
              (BEAT)
              Until he sobers up. The captain never goes down
              there. O'Leary can sober up without getting
              caught. And we don't talk about this again. It
              never happened. Now if everybody knows their
              jobs, let's get on with it.

VASQUEZ: Thanks, sir.

SCENE 17: FLETCHER'S CABIN.
SOFT SNORING. A TAP AT THE DOOR.

FLETCHER: Come in.

FX: DOOR OPENS. FOOTSTEPS ENTER.

FELTCHER: Captain.

BLAKE: Don't bother standing. Not watching your
              messages from home?

FLETCHER: I don't have any. No family left.

BLAKE: It must be hard for you handing them out to the
              crew.

FLETCHER: It's not too bad. I wish my parents were still alive
              but wishing won't bring them back. Seeing how
              much the messages cheer the crew up makes it
              worthwhile.

BLAKE: I was harsh with you yesterday, and I'm sorry for
              that.

FLETCHER: I'll get by.

BLAKE: My wife, Mary, sent me messages. So did my
              children. Did you know I've been married thirty
              years this year. It's also thirty years since I
              graduated from the Academy. Mary and I were
              married two days after I left the Academy. Three
              days after that I set out on my first ship. I didn't
              get back for eighteen months. Then it was three
              months at home and away for another year. In
              thirty years, I've spent less than four years at
              home. My children barely know me. And you
              know what I regret, John? Nothing. Our job is to
              improve the future for our children and by God
              we will. Anyway, I've taken enough of your time.

FLETCHER: No problem.
              (PAUSE)
              This picture. Beautiful. Where is it ?

FLETCHER: Montana, 300 years ago. Before we completely
              ruined the planet.

BLAKE: If we can find a place like this, all our suffering
              and sacrifices will have been worthwhile.

FLETCHER: I wonder if anywhere like that exists now.

SCENE 18. INFIRMARY. PRESENT
FLETCHER AND BLAKE.

BLAKE: There. I was stretching out my hand to you.

FLETCHER: Were you? Really? Or were you just trying to
              justify actions you knew were wrong?

BLAKE: No! I thought of you as a friend and I wanted you
              to understand how much this mission meant. Not

only to me but to the people at home relying on us. To make you see that it was worth the crew suffering a few hardships.

FLETCHER: Maybe I'd have agreed – but it wasn't just the crew for long, was it?

BLAKE: The freighter.

FLETCHER: As soon as we picked up the Quatermain's distress call it changed. It wasn't just about the crew and the mission any more.

BLAKE: Not for you, that's for sure.

SCENE 19. HANGAR BAY.
METAL SCRAPING ON METAL. CREAKING.

FLETCHER: Steady, Vasquez.

BLAKE: A ship like Endeavour wasn't built for this kind of delicate manoeuvring, John. With the Quatermain's engines dead, we have to do the hard work of bringing her into the hangar bay.

FLETCHER: I'm amazed the Quatermain made it this far. This would be a lot easier if her docking port wasn't a write-off.

BLAKE: If is a very big word, Mr Fletcher.

FX: MORE METAL CREAKS.

FLETCHER: He's cutting it fine to starboard.

BLAKE: He is that.

FLETCHER: He's the best in the fleet. If anybody can do this he can.

BLAKE: If? You didn't have any doubts when you suggested bringing the Quatermain aboard.

FLETCHER: I wasn't this close to the action before.

FX: HEAVY THUD.

FLETCHER: She's aboard. Closing outer doors. Brilliant, Vasquez. Absolutely brilliant.

BLAKE: Fine work, Mr Vasquez. Top class.

FLETCHER: The deck will be repressurised in 4, 3, 2… 1.

FX: DOOR OPENS. FOOTSTEPS GO THROUGH. HAND SLAPS METAL.

BLAKE: It's a tighter fit than I thought. The hatch should be over here. It'll be just over a metre up. There it is.

FX: METAL HATCH CLANGS OPEN.

ELENA: Captain Blake ?

BLAKE: At your service. What assistance do you need?

ELENA: We've got about a dozen casualties – a couple of them are pretty bad.

FLETCHER: Doc, you're on.

ELENA: Jake, show the doctor to the casualties.

FX: ELENA DROPS TO THE DECK.

ELENA: You'll never know how relieved I was to hear your voice. We thought we were done. I'm Elena Baxter.

BLAKE: My first officer, Mr Fletcher.

FLETCHER: Are you captain of this ship?

ELENA: I suppose I am, by default. We lost most of the
              actual crew in the accident. The power system
              developed a glitch and when we dropped under
              light speed we flew straight into a meteor shower.

BLAKE: Mr Fletcher, I want a preliminary report by
              twenty two hundred today. Miss Baxter, we will
              give whatever assistance we can.

ELENA: Thank you, captain.

FX: FOOTSTEPS HEAD AWAY.

FLETCHER: How bad is it ?

ELENA: Come aboard. See for yourself.

FX: SOUNDS OF THEM CLIMBING ABOARD THE
QUATERMAIN.

PATIENT: (WEAK)
              Help me, doctor. I can't breathe properly.

FLOWER: Coolant poisoning. I'll have you moved to
              sickbay.

ELENA: So what do you think, Mr Fletcher?

FLETCHER: The air's awful.

ELENA: We lost most of the atmospheric controls when
              we were holed. One of the techs rigged this, but
              it's been pretty unpleasant.

FLOWER: Fourteen of these people will have to go to the
              infirmary for treatment.

FLETCHER: Carry on. If you need extra space you can have
              the bunks from the men we lost.

FX: FOOTSTEPS MOVE ON.

FLETCHER: How many of you are aboard ?

ELENA: Seventeen died, so there are fifty-one of us left.
              Those who weren't hurt have been trying to keep
              the ship running as best we could. All in all,
              we've been in space just over a year.

FLETCHER: How did you manage? Ships like this are only
              supposed to carry a crew of a dozen.

ELENA: It has been a little cramped.

FLETCHER: What were you doing out here anyway ?

ELENA: We're colonists. We're heading for...
              (SHE SEEMS EMBARRASSED)
              ...Burton's Planet. I know you're going to say it's
              an old sailor's story, but our captain knew where
              it was. He was sure it was real.

FLETCHER: A habitable Earth-like planet in deep space. He
              convinced you it was real?

ELENA: He didn't have to convince me. He was my father.
              And he was one of the first to die.

FLETCHER: I'm sorry.

ELENA: So am I.

FLETCHER: Once the doc's finished with the casualties he
              should give the rest of your people a check. It'll
              give the engineers a chance to look the ship over
              in peace.

ELENA: Sounds fine to me. What do we call you? Mr
              Fletcher?

FLETCHER: John. My name's John.

ELENA: Elena.

SCENE 20: CAPTAIN'S CABIN.
BLAKE GETTING THE REPORTS. PAPERS FLICKED
THROUGH.

BLAKE: Fifty-one survivors, Mr Fletcher?

FLETCHER: Fifty. Another one died a few minutes ago. Burns.
              Our engineers say they can fix most of the
              damage but the navigation system's finished. So
              is their long-range communication.

BLAKE: She's not space-worthy, you mean. Our luck has
              been nothing but bad on this voyage, John.

FLETCHER: Should I have Vasquez turn us about and head for
              home?

BLAKE: Turn us about ? No, Mr Fletcher, you should not.
              We will continue on for the Capella system as
              planned.

FLETCHER: What about the colonists?

BLAKE: They are looking for a planet to colonise? We
              shall take them to one. They shall fulfil their
              mission as shall we. Until we make the Capella
              system, the colonists will be integrated into the
              ship's crew. They will earn their keep.

FLETCHER: And if we don't find a habitable planet?

BLAKE: I will not hear talk of failure, Mr Fletcher. I will
              not hear it. We will find these people a home.
              Have the colonists issued with uniforms and
              identification. And if they do not like it, then that
              will just be too bad for them. They will work their
              passage whether they like it or not. See to it.
              Now, Mr Fletcher, now.

31

SCENE 21: MESS HALL.
PEOPLE EATING.

O'LEARY: Vasquez, my boy. Do you see what old O'Leary
                sees?

VASQUEZ: Colonists? Refugees?

O'LEARY: Lady colonists and refugees. And some of them
                worthy of the O'Leary charm.

VASQUEZ: Haven't they had enough bad luck?

SCENE 22: INFIRMARY.
FLETCHER WAITS FOR ELENA.

FLETCHER: Well? How did your medical go?

ELENA: Apparently, I'm as healthy as a... well, something
                that's really healthy.

FLETCHER: It's unbelievable. Apart from the serious
                casualties, your people are in good shape.

ELENA: You've got to be tough to colonise a planet. Some
                are a bit put out at being press-ganged by your
                captain, but in general we're grateful to be alive
                so we'll work.

FLETCHER: I'm not sure what work we have for a botanist
                like yourself but I'll find something for you to do.
                Maybe helping to smooth the integration of the
                colonists?

ELENA: Do I have to salute?

FLETCHER: No, but you do have to wear that uniform.

ELENA: Fine. Or is it "fine, sir" ?

FLETCHER: Any more cheek and you're on a charge. Come on. We've got a lot to do.

FX: FOOTSTEPS APPROACH.

ELENA: Behave. It's the boss. Captain Blake.

BLAKE: Miss Baxter. Well, Mr Fletcher, how are we progressing?

FLETCHER: We've found work for most of the colonists. But we do have a few problems. The Endeavour was never meant to carry this many people. The atmosphere recycling units are already working at 110% safe capacity.

BLAKE: Go on.

FLETCHER: We're going to be tight for water and food. Most of the Quatermain's supplies were ruined so our provisions will be stretched to feed everybody.

FX: PAPERS HANDED OVER.

BLAKE: We still have enough for the journey but we shall have to make do will smaller rations.

FLETCHER: Elena, Miss Baxter, did have an idea.

ELENA: We're carrying a selections of seeds for high-yield plants that have been genetically engineered for accelerated growth.

BLAKE: Hardly surprising. You are a colony ship.

ELENA: We also have some nutrient-rich soil. If we plant the seeds now we'd have the first fresh food in three weeks.

BLAKE: Interesting notion. Where would you plant the seeds?

FLETCHER: Bay one's doing nothing. The only problem would be water. Even when the Quatermain's recycling systems are repaired and supplementing our own, we'd have to cut the crew's daily rations by 22%. Alternatively, we could shift power from the drive unit to the recycling system to give us more water.

BLAKE: And lose time? No, Mr Fletcher, I think not. Hold our speed constant. Cut the crew's food and water rations by 40%.

FLETCHER: But…

BLAKE: 40% is what I say and 40% is what I mean. Miss Baxter, you shall have all the water you need for your plants. By comparison with our predecessors on sailing ships 600 years ago, we shall still be spoiled. Dismissed.

FLETCHER: Yes, captain.

BLAKE MOVES AWAY. DOOR OPENS AND CLOSES BEHIND HIM. ELENA AND FLETCHER ALSO WALK OFF.

ELENA: Maybe this wasn't such a good idea.

FLETCHER: It's not the idea that's wrong. I'd better tell the crew. You never know. Pots' cooking is so bad they might even thank me.

SCENE 23. INFIRMARY. PRESENT.
BLAKE AND FLETCHER.

BLAKE: You openly questioned my orders to the Baxter woman.

FLETCHER: You were listening?

BLAKE: Eavesdropping is the word you are trying not to use. Yes, I listened. And I heard my XO question my orders – for what? To impress the woman? To gain her good favour.

FLETCHER: My… association with her is none of your business.

BLAKE: It's happening on my ship. That makes it my business, sir. And I wonder, were you trying to charm the woman or was it something more insidious? Were you trying to gain support from the colonists as well as the crew?

FLETCHER: I didn't want support from anyone. Not then and I don't want it now.

BLAKE: So you say. But you had alienated me from the crew, hadn't you? Even when I tried to join the crew for a meal, I was unwelcome.

SCENE 24: MESS HALL.
SOUNDS OF EATING.

ELENA: Well, that was... quick. The crews seem to be integrating well enough. At least that's one way of describing what I caught Kate and your Mr Croft doing last night. I haven't got him into trouble have I, John?

FLETCHER: As long as it doesn't interfere with his work, I've no objection to crewmembers... integrating.

ELENA: Good. I'm heading down to see how your techs are getting on with converting the hangar bay. Care to keep a lady company?

FLETCHER: Are you flirting with me?

ELENA: If I am?

FLETCHER: Don't want you getting lost, do we? Shall we go?

FOOTSTEPS TO DOOR. DOOR OPENS. NOISE LEVEL
DROPS IMMEDIATELY.

FLETCHER: Captain. Is there a problem, sir?

BLAKE: No, Mr Fletcher. I thought I would eat with the
              crew today, that is all. Are you finished?

FLETCHER: Yes. We're just going to check progress in the
              hangar.

BLAKE: It can't be helped. Carry on. Mr Patton. If you
              please.

POTS: Here you are, captain.

BLAKE: Thank you, Mr Patton. It looks splendid.
              Splendid.

FX: UNCOMFORTABLE SILENCE.

BLAKE: Continue your meals, gentlemen. Don't let my
              presence interrupt.
              (TRYING TOO HARD)
              Settling in? Good. Good.
              (EATING)
              Excellent as always, Mr Patton.

FX: IT'S AN UNCOMFORTABLE ATMOSPHERE AND
GETTING MORE SO. IT'S GETTING TO BLAKE.

BLAKE: Please carry on as if I were not here.

FX: BLAKE CONTINUES EATING. CUTLERY SCRAPING
ON THE PLATE.

BLAKE: Please, continue with your meals. I insist. Carry
              on.

FINISHES MEAL.

BLAKE: First rate meal, Mr Patton.

FX: BLAKE WALKS OUT. DOOR CLOSES.

O'LEARY: It's bad enough that he's starving us. Does he have to come and gloat about it as well? He hasn't killed any of us in weeks. Maybe starvation's how he's going to get the rest of us.

VASQUEZ: Quiet, he'll hear you.

SCENE 25. SHUTTLE BAY.
LEAVES BEING SPRAYED.

FLETCHER: I can't believe it. Those things have only been in a few days, Elena.

ELENA: Am I good or what? These plants will be ready in twenty-three days. Wish I knew exactly what they are. They're not tagged yet. They'll be fresh, though. But I'm sure your cook will still manage to ruin them. Have you been in the Corps long?

FLETCHER: Sixteen years, give or take. Career military. Unless something better comes along.

ELENA: That's fair. I wonder if there's a way we can improve the drainage.

FLETCHER: Drainage, eh? You know how to sweet talk a man. Who can resist a woman who talks about drainage?

ELENA: I didn't know you were trying to resist me.

FLETCHER: Sure of yourself, aren't you?

ELENA: In truth? No. It's all bravado.

FLETCHER: It's working.

SCENE 26. ENDEAVOUR ENGINEERING.
CLANKING MACHINERY. DOOR OPENS. PETERS,
AUSTRALIAN ENGINEER IS THERE.

PETERS: Captain Blake. We don't often see you down here
               in engineering, sir.

BLAKE: Mr Peters, there's a mystery in these water levels.
               Can you explain it?

PETERS: No, sir but I'll get onto it as soon as I finish up.

BLAKE: That's not good enough. We've already lost more
               than four litres. We will look into it now. The
               problem is in H7, according to this.

FX: FOOTSTEPS.

PETERS: The lads and me can do this, captain.

BLAKE: No, thank you. I am quite capable.

FX: DOOR OPENS. SHRIEK FROM A WOMAN AND FROM
O'LEARY.

BLAKE: Mr O'Leary, what in the Hell is this ?

O'LEARY: Oh, God.

BLAKE: This is where the water has gone? You've stolen
               the ship's water to make alcohol in this still? And
               you use my ship for this fornication?

FX: METAL ROD GRABBED, GLASS SMASHED
VIOLENTLY. BLAKE LOSES CONTROL.

BLAKE: No more. NO MORE !

PETERS: (ON COMM)
               Mr Fletcher...

FLETCHER: (ON COMM)
              Fletcher here. What on earth…

PETERS: You'd better get to H7 straight away, sir.

FX: RAMPAGE OF SMASHING CONTINUES.

BLAKE: You will make no more. No more of this filth. No
              more I say. Not on my ship.

FX: FOOTSTEPS RUN IN.

FLETCHER: What the devil's happening ?

BLAKE: That man has stolen precious water from his
              shipmates and made this filth. But you must have
              told others. Who else knew about this? Who
              knew? Who? Answer me, damn you. Who knew?

O'LEARY: (SHOCKED BY BLAKE'S LOSS OF
              CONTROL)
              Nobody.

BLAKE: Nobody, SIR. Say it!

O'LEARY: Nobody, sir.

BLAKE: Liar! You are a thief and a liar and a fornicator.
              You disgust me. Get him out of here. Put that filth
              in the brig. He will stay there until we make the
              Capella system. No visitors. He has stolen water,
              so he will do without until he has made up the
              loss. Put him on survival rations only. Minimal
              food and water. Discipline on this ship has gone
              to the devil and do you know who I blame? You,
              Mr Fletcher, that is who. You are first officer and
              it is you who should set the tone for the crew to
              follow, but you are more interested in being their
              friend than their superior officer. Well, things will
              change, mark my words. Oh, yes, they will
              change. First of all, female colonists will be

moved into quarters aboard the Quatermain.
When not on duty, they will be confined to their
own ship. I will not have this behaviour on my
ship. Discipline, that is what is needed. In
addition to their duties, the men will have two
hour-long periods of strenuous exercise every
day. They will not meet or talk to these women
except when required to do so by their duties and
I will have an armed guard on the Quatermain at
all times. Other than the women, only you and I
shall have access to their ship. Well? What are
you waiting for?

FX: BLAKE STORMS OUT. SHOCKED SILENCE FOR A
MOMENT.

FLETCHER: Get this place cleaned up.

ELENA: You want to talk about that? He was completely
out of control.

FLETCHER: I don't want to hear it, Elena. You'd better pass
the captain's orders to the other women.

ELENA: John, he lost control.

FLETCHER: I don't want to hear it!

ELENA: I'll pass the word to the others. They won't be
happy.

FLETCHER: We don't get paid to be happy.

ELENA: We don't get paid.

SCENE 27. BLAKE'S QUARTERS.
BLAKE ENTERS. SLAMS DOOR SHUT.

BLAKE: Mary, they are all against me. They do not have
the strength of character to carry this task through

to the finish. But I am the captain and I will lead them through. They will not make me fail. I will not fail.

SCENE 28. INFIRMARY. PRESENT.
BLAKE AND FLETCHER.

FLETCHER: You're paranoid. The crew aren't against you.

BLAKE: No?

FLETCHER: Not then anyway. You turned them against you.

BLAKE: You must take responsibility for that.

FLETCHER: No! You did that by yourself. You cut their rations. You kept half of them locked away in the Quatermain. You made them do two hours of physical exercise every day on top of longer work shifts. You made the engineers wear full uniform in temperatures over 120 degrees. You did all that and a damn sight more.

BLAKE: Discipline, that is the key.

FLETCHER: That's not discipline. It's blatant, inhuman cruelty. You locked yourself away from the crew, hiding in your cabin. I was with them every day. I watched morale go through the floor and there was nothing I could do to stop it.

SCENE 29: MESS HALL.
FLOWER AND FLETCHER TALKING. THE CREW ARE
RUMBLING UNHAPPILY.

FLOWER: I didn't think Pots' cooking could get any worse, John. From a professional point of view, John, it's short on nutrition and it tastes like pig-swill. It's not doing morale any good. And the mental health of the crew is part of my job so don't lecture me for interfering.

FLETCHER: This is a tough job, Doc. We knew that when we signed up.

FLOWER: The colonists didn't sign up. They didn't ask to be jailed in that ship of theirs either. And in my professional opinion, it's not doing you any good either. You've been a misery for the past month since the captain put a stop to you and Elena.

FLETCHER: What about me and Elena?

FLOWER: I'm not blind. I can see how you look at her. And how you avoid looking at her. She's got it as bad as you.

FLETCHER: That your medical opinion?

FLOWER: It's your friend's opinion. But you answer me honestly, do you think we're right to carry on this mission?

FX: NO REPLY.

FLOWER: That's what I thought. You only have to look at the crew to know what they think.

SCENE 30. INT. BRIG.
O'LEARY IS SINGING TO HIMSELF.

O'LEARY: As I was going over, the Cork and Kerry mountains…

DOOR OPENS.

O'LEARY: Mr Fletcher.

FLETCHER: O'Leary. How are you doing?

O'LEARY: Hungry. And I'd kill for a drink of water. Does this mean I'm getting out? Though from what I hear I'm probably better off in here.

FLETCHER: I thought you weren't supposed to get any visitors. Then again, I'm not supposed to be here either. We all knew about your still. If you'd told the captain, he'd have gone easier on you. Especially as I knew.

O'LEARY: When I got drunk before, you could have thrown me in here for a month, reported me... You didn't. I owed you.

FLETCHER: I heard you'd had a hard time. I tried to talk the captain into letting you out but he wasn't interested.

O'LEARY: It's not your fault I'm in here. Don't beat yourself up.

FX: SOUND OF PARCEL BEING THROWN.

FLETCHER: We reach the Capella system in a couple of days. You get out then. This'll keep you fed till then.

FX: DOOR CLOSES. PARCEL OPENED.

O'LEARY: Fresh fruit? You have been busy out there.

SCENE 31: INT. QUATERMAIN.
KNOCK AT A DOOR.

ELENA: What is it now? Chloe, if it's the power relay in your cabin, move somewhere else till tomorrow.

FX: DOOR OPENS AND CLOSES.

ELENA: John. If you're looking for the update on the plants you'll have it tomorrow.

FLETCHER: I'm not here about the plants.
(A BIT UNCOMFORTABLE)
The captain. He picked me for this mission, you know. Made me first officer when we lost the

XO. He's a good man really. A good captain. He has one of the best records in the Corps.

ELENA: And that's why you're loyal to him, even when he acting like he is. Nobody's infallible, John. He makes mistakes like everybody else.

FLETCHER: Only because he determined to find us a new planet to colonise.

ELENA: Sit down. It isn't determination, John. It's obsession. It's dangerous – and you know it.

FLETCHER: I know. I don't want to go against his orders. He's my friend. I owe him. But some of his orders I can't follow. I won't stay away from you. Unless you want me to.

ELENA: Stay. Here, tonight.

FX: SOUNDS OF A KISS.

FLETCHER: He'd skin us alive if he found out.

ELENA: Sssh.

SCENE 32: INT. CAPTAIN'S CABIN.
BLAKE IS MUTTERING AND MUMBLING, RESTLESS.
MUTED SOUND FROM OUTSIDE. HE WAKES SUDDENLY.

BLAKE: Who's there?
(BEAT – NO ANSWER)
Computer, this is the captain. Lock my cabin door. At once. Immediately.

FX: SOUND OF GUN BEING COCKED.

SCENE 33. ELENA'S CABIN.
SOUND OF DRESSING.

ON THE SHELF

ELENA: Do you have to go, Mr Fletcher, Sir? I preferred it
            when the clothes were coming off.

FLETCHER: So did I. Enjoying the floorshow? Where's my
            boot?
            (BEAT)
            Is this real?

ELENA: It was my mother's. She got it from her
            grandmother.

FX: DRAWS FINGERS OVER GUITAR STRINGS –
HORRIBLY OUT OF TUNE.

ELENA: I'm too scared of breaking the strings to try
            tuning them. It's real wood, though. The fret-
            board's almost worn through but it's real.

FLETCHER: Incredible. I'd better go. I'll see you in a while.

ELENA: Okay.

FX: A KISS. DOOR CLOSES. GUITAR STRUMMED
THOUGHTFULLY.

SCENE 34. INFIRMARY. PRESENT.
BLAKE AND FLETCHER.

BLAKE: The day we arrived at Capella 3 I released
            O'Leary, as I had said I would. I am a man of my
            word. I told him that he had committed a crime
            but that I would not hold it against him and I sent
            him to join the crew for a meal. Do you know
            what he said, Mr Fletcher? No, of course you
            don't – you were nowhere to be found.

FLETCHER: I was working.

BLAKE: Working indeed. I shall tell you what he said. "No
            thank you, captain. I'm not hungry." That is what
            he said. Someone had been feeding him. Who

would that have been, I wonder?

FLETCHER: He's got a lot of friends in the crew.

BLAKE: I hear they gave him quite the reception in the mess hall. A returning hero.

FLETCHER: Some see him that way.

BLAKE: How do you see him, John? Tell me that.

FLETCHER: He's a trouble-maker. Always has been.

BLAKE: And yet you have brought us to this for him and his kind. Is he worth it, John? Is he?

SCENE 35. FLIGHT DECK.
SHIP IN FULL OPERATION.

FLETCHER: Probes away.

BLAKE: Send them on their way, Mr Fletcher. I have a feeling that Capella 3 is about to change our luck. Good. Good. Put their transmission on screen.

FLETCHER: Probes entering the atmosphere. Pressure – point 96 of Earth. Nitrogen 71%, Oxygen 25%, the rest is various inert gasses. Gravity point 91 of Earth. Nothing toxic.

BLAKE: Splendid. Miss Baxter, what do you make of it?

ELENA: It's perfect.

BLAKE: (ALMOST RELIGIOUS – VINDICATED.) Clean oceans, untainted air. It's paradise. We have done it. We have found an Eden for our people.

FLETCHER: Captain, I've got something on Probe 4. I'm putting it on screen.

FX: A MOMENT – BUTTONS PRESSED.

FLETCHER: Primates. Corps rules prohibit colonisation of planets with intelligent, indigenous life.

ELENA: And they count?

FLETCHER: Yes.

BLAKE: No, they do not. They are animals, sir. Animals. And I will not be denied by animals. Mr Miller, prepare the shuttle. We are going to that planet. Break out the weapons. If those things get in our path we will gun them down. Wipe them out.

FLETCHER: (LOW, URGENT)
You can't do this, William.

BLAKE: Can't? Who are you to tell me what I cannot do? What of our own people's right to live?

FLETCHER: These creatures have a right to live. If you kill them, you'll be breaking the rules you've followed all your life. You'll regret it as long as you live. Look at them. They have fire. They have tools. They make tools. They are us, fifty thousand years ago. What if someone had wiped us out?

BLAKE: (STRUGGLING TO PULL HIMSELF TOGETHER)
You're right, of course. Belay that last order, Mr Miller. Mr Fletcher, take the shuttle down and replenish our provisions. I'm sorry, Miss Baxter. It seems that you won't be colonising Burton's Planet after all.

ELENA: We gave up on Burton's Planet a long time ago, captain. According to our charts it's another three light years past here anyway.

47

BLAKE: I shall be in my quarters.

FX: FOOTSTEPS GO.

FLETCHER: Miss Baxter. I need a botanist – are you up to the
                job?

ELENA: Yes, sir.

SCENE 36. ENDEAVOUR.

CREWMAN: Captain.

BLAKE: Out of my way, man.

FX: DOOR OPENS AND CLOSES. ALONE, BLAKE IS
FALLING APART. HE SCREAMS AND YELLS AND
WRECKS THE ROOM.

BLAKE: No! I will not give in. I will not fail!

SCENE 37: EXT. CAPELLA 3.
SOUNDS OF WIND IN TREES AND LONG GRASS. SOME
BIRD CALLS AS WELL.

FLETCHER: This is a new planet, so check in every hour and
                be back here in six hours. No interactions with the
                natives and don't eat anything till it's been
                checked out. Miss Baxter, you're with me. This
                way looks promising.

ELENA: This planet would have been perfect. It's what
                Earth used to be. Real plants – this is even a grass
                of some sort. Perfect.
                (BEAT)
                When the rest are out of sight want to break the
                rules again?

FLETCHER: We have work to do, loose woman.

ELENA: (A MOMENT'S HESITATION THEN)
        The captain is unstable.

FLETCHER: He wouldn't have gone through with killing those
           creatures. He was just... disappointed. We'll be
           heading back to Earth now. It's an easy trip.
           Boring, but easy. If there's a problem with the
           captain, they'll find it when we get home. He's
           my friend – was my friend. I owe him. That
           doesn't mean I won't break some of his rules.

ELENA: Oh. That does sound promising...

SCENE 38. CAPTAIN'S CABIN.
WILD SCRABBLING OF PAPERS.

BLAKE: Not Burton. Not Burton's Planet, she said. Charts.
        I must have my charts.

SCENE 39. ENDEAVOUR.
DOOR OPENS.

COMPUTER: Shuttle deck repressurised.

O'LEARY: Home sweet home.

FLETCHER: You love it, O'Leary.

O'LEARY: I liked the planet better.

FLETCHER: Pity the primates got there first. Get something to
           eat then put a crew together to unload the shuttle.

FX: FOOTSTEPS TRUDGE OFF. OTHER FOOTSTEPS
HURRY TOWARDS THEM.

MILLER: Mr Fletcher, the captain wants you on the flight
         deck. You as well, Miss Baxter.

FLETCHER: We'll be there in a few minutes, Miller.

SCENE 40. MESS HALL.
A HUSHED CONVERSATION.

O'LEARY: I know it's dangerous but so is staying on this
             ship. If we take the shuttle down to the planet we
             can hide out and live peacefully. Between the
             crew and colonists, I count at least forty of us
             who'd be ready to go. The captain will go berserk.
             Let him. We'd have the only shuttle. He wouldn't
             be able to come down after us. I don't know about
             you but I don't want to spend another year on this
             ship going back to Earth. And why would the
             colonists want to go back at all? We all spent long
             enough trying to get away from there. Come on.
             Say you're with us.

FLETCHER: If you do, you're on a charge.

O'LEARY: Mr Fletcher, we were just...

FLETCHER: Plotting a mutiny by the sound of it. Just as well
             Elena suggested we eat as well.

O'LEARY: It's not mutiny. Just the chance to be human
             again. On a real planet. I saw how you looked at
             that planet down there. It could be a real home.
             Come with us.

FLETCHER: Understand this, all of you. If any of you try to
             jump ship, I'll kick your heads off your shoulders
             and throw what's left in the brig personally. I was
             going to up your break to six hours before
             unloading the shuttle. I think you'd better get on
             with it now. And there'll be an armed guard on
             the shuttle just in case.

SCENE 41. FLIGHT DECK.
BLAKE WITH FLOWER.

BLAKE: Your reports show the crew in reasonable health,
             Doctor Flower.

FLOWER:	They could be a better. A lot better.
BLAKE:	All things considered, they are in fine shape.

FX: DOOR OPENS

BLAKE:	Mr Fletcher. We are all safely aboard, I assume.
FLETCHER:	With plenty of provisions, captain.
BLAKE:	Splendid. Mr Vasquez, set a new course. 7-7-1-4-8-2-2 by 9-3-6.
FLETCHER:	We're going on?
BLAKE:	Of course we are going onwards. Miss Baxter, we are taking you to Burton's Planet. I downloaded your father's logs from the Quatermain and read them. There's more than enough proof in them to convince me of the planet's existence.
ELENA:	But we can't be certain it's there.
FLETCHER:	Even if we were sure, we don't have the fuel to find Burton's Planet and get back to earth.
BLAKE:	On our return journey we shall send a message ahead and have a ship meet us with extra fuel. Our duty is to find new planets to colonise. My duty is to save those billions on Earth.
FLETCHER:	What good is that if everyone on this ship is dead, William? Who'll send the call to Earth? Who'll tell them?
BLAKE:	We go on. That is my decision.
FLETCHER:	No.
BLAKE:	What did you say? What did you say, sir? Repeat it.

FLETCHER: I said "no". We will not go on.

BLAKE: You will do as I say! Or are you disobeying a
              direct order form a superior officer? Your
              commanding officer.

FLETCHER: If you insist on this course of action I must
              question your fitness for command and as first
              officer demand that the doctor conduct a
              psychiatric evaluation.

BLAKE: So you are part of this as well, doctor. So you
              plan to be rid of me. Well, we should get on with
              this, shouldn't we? You will find, that I am in full
              command of all of my faculties and when that is
              recorded in your log, we shall indeed go on. I
              need no time to prepare myself. We will do the
              evaluation now and be rid of this foolishness.

FX: FOOTSTEPS HEAD OFF.

ELENA: John?

FLETCHER: What have I done?

SCENE 42. INFIRMARY. PRESENT.
BLAKE AND FLETCHER.

BLAKE: Indeed, Mr Fletcher. What have you done? You
              will take responsibility for this evaluation. As
              executive officer, you must.

FLETCHER: I was within my rights to ask that your fitness be
              queried.

BLAKE: I know regulations, damn you! But it doesn't
              matter, does it? What happens if your doctor says
              I am not fit to command? We shall turn back to
              Earth, I know that, for you are a coward. After
              that? You're too young for a command of your
              own and who will take you as XO? A man who

turned on his captain? One of the most respected captains in the Corps, if I may say. No-one, Mr Fletcher, that is who. No-one. No-one will have as XO a man who betrayed his captain and who is afraid of the challenge of exploration. You will be lucky to find a position as a navigator on a fright barge between Mars and the asteroid belt.

FLETCHER: At least I'll have saved these people. If I'm drummed out of the Corps, maybe I'll farm a frontier world,

BLAKE: You're not a farmer, John. You're a sailor, like me. You could never bear to be in one place all your days. Even with the Baxter woman. Oh, I've noticed you and her and I've let it pass.

FLETCHER: You may be right.

BLAKE: At least one of us is finished. Will it be one or both, I wonder.

FLETCHER: You once told me there was no malice in nature. Just the urge to survive. I'm just trying to make sure that we all survive.

FX: DOOR OPENS.

BLAKE: Well, doctor? You have the results?

FLOWER: Yes.

FLETCHER: What do they say?

BLAKE: I will give the order to release the results. I am still captain, am I not? Doctor, if you please, you will read out the results in the presence of the ship's crew. I have given orders that they assemble in the mess.

SCENE 43. MESS HALL.
RUMBLE OF ANTICIPATION.

O'LEARY: I'll say this for him he's got guts.

BLAKE: We all know why we're here. I see no sense in dragging this out. Doctor, the results of your tests, if you will.

FLOWER: As... well, as required by regulations, I conducted a psychological evaluation of Captain Blake. He is suffering from stress, resulting in high blood pressure, lack of sleep and various related symptoms. His answers to my questions also showed him to be unhealthily obsessive with regard to his work. He is also suffering from a form of depression.

FX: CHEERING FROM THE CREW.

FLETCHER: However, according to my examinations, while he would not be fit to work some heavy machinery on Earth, the captain is marginally within the limits considered acceptable for command by Corps regulations. My findings, as bound by the Corps' regulations, are that Captain Blake is fit for command.

FX: HORRIFIED REACTION FROM CREW.

BLAKE: Mr Fletcher, have a course set for Burton's Planet. Light speed four. Immediately, Mr Fletcher.
(GLOATING BEAT)
I didn't hear your answer, Mr Fletcher. Speak up.

FLETCHER: Yes, captain.

O'LEARY: No.

BLAKE: What did you say Mr O'Leary?

O'LEARY: No. I'm not going any further. You've starved us, worked us like dogs and treated us like animals. I've had enough. We all have.

FX: SOUND OF GUN BEING COCKED.

O'LEARY: I'll kill you where you stand rather than go another metre.

BLAKE: Put the gun down, Mr O'Leary.

O'LEARY: I'm not taking your orders any more. And I'm not the only one. More than half the crew has had enough. You're not giving orders any more.

FLETCHER: Don't do it, O'Leary. He's not worth it.

O'LEARY: After what he's done to all of us? I think he's worth it.

FLETCHER: Don't be stupid, O'Leary. Listen to me. It's…

FX: SOUND OF A SCUFFLE AND THE GUN BEING GRABBED.

FLETCHER: Give me that. Idiot!

BLAKE: Thank you, Mr Fletcher. A most timely intervention. Mr O'Leary, you have crossed me for the last time. You tried to kill me. In front of all of these witnesses no less. Well, no more, I say. No more. There will be no need for a court martial. A captain's word is law. Your actions are punishable by the death penalty and that is what we shall have. Mr Miller, take two men and space this man.
             (NOTHING)
             Mr Miller, I said take this man and eject him into space. Do it! DO IT!

FLETCHER: Don't move, Miller. I won't let you throw him into space. It's inhuman.

BLAKE: I am captain. You will do as I say.

FLETCHER: Not this time.

BLAKE: Is this mutiny, Mr Fletcher? Is it?

FLETCHER: If mutiny's what it takes to save this man's life...

FX: GUN COCKED.

FLETCHER: ... then it's mutiny.

FX: SHOCKED SILENCE – THEN CHEERS.

BLAKE: Mutiny. You know what that means?

FLETCHER: Shut up.

O'LEARY: Shoot him Kill him.

FX: A VIOLENT BLOW AND A PAINED REACTION FROM O'LEARY.

FLETCHER: There will be no killing. Not you, not him.

BLAKE: You don't have the stomach for this.

FLETCHER: Shut up. Shut up or I swear I'll blow your brains all over that wall myself.

BLAKE: Put the gun down and we can forget this.

FLETCHER: It's gone too far for that and we both know it.

BLAKE: If any of you stand along with this man, you will be declaring yourselves outlaws. Stand with me and we can take the ship. Who is with me and who is a traitor?

FLETCHER: (THOUGHTFUL – TO CROWD)
He's right. If you're with me, you'll be an outlaw. You'll never be able to go back to Earth. We'll be outcasts. If you have family, you won't see them again. Choose carefully. There won't be any turning back. Peters, you're going to be a grandfather. Think about it. Vasquez, you're getting married. Think about it, all of you. If you're not with me, you won't be harmed. O'Leary, anyone who's with the captain – keep them locked in here. If any of them are hurt, you answer to me.

FX: FLETCHER STOMPS OUT.

ELENA: John. Stop, John.

FLETCHER: I didn't want this.

ELENA: I know, but you couldn't let him commit murder. Even if it was O'Leary.

FLETCHER: Now half the crew is ready to murder the other half.

ELENA: The colonists will back you. I'm sure of that. What are you going to do with Blake? You'll have to come up with something quickly – before O'Leary takes matters into his own hands.

FLETCHER: I know. O'Leary wants Blake dead. Maybe I should confine Blake to the Quatermain.

ELENA: That's not a bad idea.

FLETCHER: Or maybe… let's have a look at the Quatermain.

SCENE 45. SHUTTLE BAY.
MEETING BETWEEN BLAKE AND FLETCHER.

BLAKE: So those are our options, Mr Fletcher? Neither is acceptable.

FLETCHER: Too bad. You can either be put ashore on the planet below, with a distress beacon or you can take the colonists' ship and make for home in that.

BLAKE: We can be either marooned or set adrift in this wreck.

FLETCHER: Peters' repairs have made the Quatermain spaceworthy. Structurally, she's sound, but the engines are old. I can't make any promises. They're not the big problem. The navigation unit was destroyed when they were holed.

BLAKE: You'd send us out to fly blind.

FLETCHER: You always said you could navigate by the stars. The shuttle has medium range navigation for emergencies. That can be transplanted into the Quatermain. The choice is yours.

BLAKE: We shall set for home in the ship.

FLETCHER: I thought you would. The ship's provisioned with food and water for two months. After that it's up to the recycling system.

BLAKE: We will survive, never fear.

FLETCHER: I hope you do.

BLAKE: Then you are more of a fool than I thought. When the Corps finds us, they shall send a fleet of ships to hunt you down. You should have killed us.

FX: FOOTSTEPS APPROACH.

ELENA: The last of my possessions, such as they are.

FLETCHER: More than enough to have filled my cabin.

FX: DOOR OPENS. FOOTSTEPS FILE IN.

FLETCHER: Captain, your ship's waiting.

BLAKE: (STICKING IN HIS CRAW)
             Before we set off, I have a favour to ask. If I
             remember Mr Peters' repair reports, Quatermain's
             recycling unit can only provide enough air for
             twelve of us. I would be obliged if you would
             keep Mr Miller aboard.

MILLER: I don't want to stay…

BLAKE: You will obey your orders, Mr Miller. Put my
             crew aboard Quatermain. He will be unharmed?

FLETCHER: Naturally. Now I have to ask a favour. Doctor
             Flower is coming with us against his will. We
             need a doctor and he's the only one aboard.

BLAKE: So it shall be noted in my log. If that is all, we
             shall be under way. You are in command now,
             John. Enjoy it. But how long before someone here
             turns on you? We will meet again, Mr Fletcher,
             and when we do, you will dance at the end of a
             rope.

FX: METAL HATCH CLOSES.

SCENE 46. FLIGHT DECK.
MILLER REPORTS TO FLETCHER. FLIGHT DECK SOUNDS
BUSY.

MILLER: The Quatermain is free and clear.

FLETCHER: Good.
             (SOFTLY)
             Good luck.

O'LEARY: And good riddance.

FLETCHER: Chong, power up the engines. We can't stay here.

O'LEARY: Of course we can. We've got the perfect planet down there and Blake's gone.

FLETCHER: You heard him. He'll be back. If he finds us here, we're all be guilty of mutiny. The rest may be lucky and get life sentences in the Martian mines, but you and I will be at the end of ropes, O'Leary. We're going to the place Blake thinks we'd never go. Burton's planet. Lay in course.

O'LEARY: You're taking us God knows where to a planet that might not even exist.

FLETCHER: You should have thought of that before you pulled a gun on your captain. You started this, O'Leary, now this is the only chance we have. Take us out, Chong. Prepare for light speed then take us up to Light Speed by 5.

O'LEARY: The engines weren't designed to run for any length of time at over Light 4.

FLETCHER: Then you'd better get to the engine room and keep them running.

FX: FOOTSTEPS GO.

ELENA: Is that safe, John?

FLETCHER: Don't worry. The engines can go up to Light 6 with no trouble. I'm just keeping them all busy. They've mutinied once. It'll come a lot easier second time.

ELENA: Are you armed?

JOHN: Yes. I want you to carry a gun as well. Just in case.

SCENE 47. QUATERMAIN FLIGHT DECK.

BLAKE: Stand down Mr Vasquez. It's my watch.

VASQUEZ: Yes, captain.

BLAKE: Ship's log, Captain William Blake recording. It's now thirty-one days since we set out. The work is long and hard. The ship requires constant repair and attention, but given the circumstances, morale is good. I cannot commend this loyal crew highly enough.

FX: CHIRP FROM INTERCOM.

BLAKE: Go ahead.

PETERS: (ON COMM)
                    Captain, it's Peters in engineering. The power-coupling is beginning to over-heat.

BLAKE: Can you repair it ?

PETERS: No, Sir. I can't replace it either.

BLAKE: How much power will we lose if it blows?

PETERS: Everything, near as makes no odds. Light speed, heat, atmosphere recycling.

BLAKE: How long do we have ?

PETERS: Impossible to be sure, sir. It'll run till it blows. I'm sorry, captain, it's the best I can offer.

BLAKE: It can't be helped.

FX: SWITCHES OFF RADIO.

BLAKE: And we're still at least nine months shy of Earth.
(THOUGHTFUL)
We need to cut our journey time. Or the time it
takes to get word to Earth perhaps…

FX: HITS INTERCOM.

BLAKE: Mr Vasquez, to the Flight Deck. Immediately.

FX: FOOTSTEPS RUN.

VASQUEZ: Captain?

BLAKE: Alter course, Mr Vasquez. Change to 1-7-2-4-8-
6-2.

VASQUEZ: That takes us away from Earth, captain.

BLAKE: I'm aware of that.

VASQUEZ: Changing course, aye sir.

BLAKE: Extend sensor equipment, such as it is, to
maximum. We may not make it home but we will
not go quietly.

SCENE 48. ENDEAVOUR FLIGHT DECK.
FLETCHER, MILLER AND ELENA.

FLETCHER: How's recycling, Miller?

MILLER: Not as efficient as it could be but passable.

FLETCHER: Let's see. It's poor. Somebody down there's
slacking.

MILLER: Since the mutiny, most of them are slack in their
work.

ELENA: John. Company.

FLETCHER: O'Leary. What can I do for you?

O'LEARY: Me and a few of the boys were wondering how much longer till we get to this Burton's Planet?

FLETCHER: Thirteen days.

O'LEARY: It's just that if we go much further we won't have the supplies to get back to Earth's territory.

FLETCHER: We can't go back. None of us can.

O'LEARY: We can go back to Capella 3. They might not come after us. A lot of us want to go back there.

FLETCHER: You've been taking a poll? Fine. Let me at the controls, would you, Chong?

FX: BUTTONS PUNCHED.

O'LEARY: We're going back to Capella?

FLETCHER: Get it through your head, we can't go back. Not ever. We're going on to Burton's Planet. I've used command codes to lock in our destination. Our course can't be changed. We go on.

FX: GUNS COCKED.

FLETCHER: Do you have a problem with that? No? Pity. I'm sure Mr Miller here would have enjoyed shooting you. I know I would have. Elena too, probably. Now take your monkeys and get back to your stations. Move.

ELENA: It's going to get worse until we reach the planet.

FLETCHER: Don't go anywhere without your gun and don't go anywhere alone.

ELENA: What about you ?

FLETCHER: I'm staying here. If anybody wants me, they'll find me here.

SCENE 49. QUATERMAIN FLIGHT DECK.

VASQUEZ: Sensors on full. Still nothing, Captain Blake.

BLAKE: Keep looking. It has to be here somewhere.

VASQUEZ: What does? What are we looking for?

FX: AN ALARM.

VASQUEZ: There's some sort of gravitational pull ahead.

BLAKE: That's it. I knew my memory wouldn't play me false. There is no substitute for experience. A wormhole. A channel that folds space and time and makes travel time between two points shorter. This one comes out near Sirius. We have an outpost there. I remember reading the report of a ship coming across the other end of this wormhole there a while back. It's too small for us to pass though, but we can send a message home. Prepare a buoy and have my journal copied into it.

VASQUEZ: Buoy ready... journal copying... ready, sir. Buoy away. The buoy has entered the wormhole, captain.

BLAKE: Good. Now we shall have to...

PETERS: (ON COMM)
Captain, it's Peters. The relay's gone. The launch system for the buoy was too much for it.

BLAKE: It had to happen eventually. Move everyone to the centre of the ship. If we have lost heating, the centre of the ship will retain what heat we do have for longest. Mr Vasquez, we are dead in space.

> There's no need for anyone on the flight deck now. We have sent the buoy. They know where we are – and they know of Fletcher's piracy. Shut down all systems here.

SCENE 50. ENDEAVOUR FLIGHT DECK.

FLOWER: Latest medical reports, John.

ELENA: Sssh. Quiet, Doctor. He's asleep. It's the first sleep he's had in three days.

FX: DEEP, STEADY BREATHING.

FLOWER: I could give him something to make him sleep.

ELENA: He wouldn't take it. Just let him sleep here for now.

FLOWER: When did you sleep last?

ELENA: I'll sleep when he wakes up.

FLOWER: Keep your hand on that gun of yours.

ELENA: I haven't been anywhere without it for two weeks.

FLETCHER IS SLIGHTLY RESTLESS. MOANS A LITTLE IN HIS SLEEP.

ELENA: Sssh.

SCENE 51. INT. QUATERMAIN.

BLAKE: (VERY WEAKLY)
             Computer, record ship's log. Computer? Dead. Mr Vasquez, would you pass out the water rations?

VASQUEZ: (SHIVERING)
             It's frozen over, captain.

BLAKE: Break the surface. It may only be frozen on top.
Otherwise we shall just have to suck the ice.

FX: TAPPING ON THE ICE.

SCENE 52. ENDEAVOUR FLIGHT DECK.

FLETCHER: Under light speed in three, two, one... under light
speed now.

ELENA: At least there's a system here.

FLETCHER: Just as well. I see O'Leary's brought his friends.
(LOUDER)
Scan the system for planets.

MILLER: Scanning... seven planets.

FLETCHER: How many look habitable ?

MILLER: The inner three are too close to the sun. Three gas
giants a little further out and one small planet at
the edge of the system.

FLETCHER: What about that one?

MILLER: It's too far out. The atmosphere is frozen.
Probably methane. I'm sorry, John.

O'LEARY: None of them are habitable. You dragged us out
here for nothing. We should have stayed at
Capella. You've killed us all.

FX: GUN COCKED.

ELENA: Keep back, O'Leary, or I'll kill you.

FLETCHER: Elena. It doesn't matter.

O'LEARY: It matters to me. Why did we trust you? We could
have lived back on Capella. We could...

MILLER: Wait. I've got another planet. It was hidden
               behind the sun. It's just coming into view now.

FLETCHER: Is it habitable ?

MILLER: I can't tell. The sun's corona is interfering with
               the scans.

SCENE 53. INT. QUATERMAIN.
THE SHIP SOUNDS COLD AND WET AND LIKE A TOMB.

COMM: (MUFFLED, DISTORTED)
               This is the Earth cruiser Biko to the Quatermain.
               We have docked and are preparing to come
               aboard.

CLANG OF METAL DOCKING HATCH OPENING.
SHUFFLING OF FEET.

BLAKE: I am Captain William Blake of the Endeavour.
               My crew and I must report a mutiny and an act of
               piracy.

SOUND OF BLAKE COLLAPSING.

SCENE 54. INT. SPACE CORPS HQ.
THREE BELLS, STRUCK ONE AFTER THE OTHER.
ADMIRAL BAILEY SPEAKS.

BAILEY: Having heard all available evidence, this enquiry
               Into events on the Corps Deep Space exploration
               vessel, Endeavour, is ready to deliver its findings.
               There is no doubt that what happened on the
               Endeavour was indeed mutiny and the theft of the
               ship an act of piracy. Warrants will be sworn out
               for all members of the crew who did not join
               Captain Blake on the Quatermain, with the
               exceptions of Doctor Flower and Ensign Miller.
               We are aware of and stress their innocence in this
               matter. The mutineers are to be arrested on sight.
               At this time, the boards commends Captain Blake

for his extraordinary efforts in saving the lives of his crew on the Quatermain. We have no doubts that had he not been in command of that ship, the crew would surely have died in space.

BLAKE: Thank you, Admiral Bailey.

BAILEY: However, while we feel that John Fletcher was the instigator of the mutiny, Captain William Blake was guilty of errors in judgement which contributed to the deterioration of morale aboard the Endeavour, which led, at least in part, to the mutiny. This is a sad occasion. In its history of over 100 years, this is the first time the Corps has faced this kind of insurrection. The finding of this enquiry is that members of the crew of the Space Corps vessel, the Endeavour, led by Lieutenant John Fletcher, did indeed mutiny against Space Corps, as represented by Captain William Blake by disobeying direct orders, threatening a superior officer, and by stealing the said ship, Endeavour. These mutineers are declared outlaw and their property is confiscated. They will be tried for their crimes if and when they are captured. The crewmembers who returned with Captain Blake are each given official commendations and where appropriate, promotion. They have the option of returning to duty or retiring due to their injuries at full salary. Captain Blake will retain his current rank and will be reassigned to a post here at Corps HQ.

BLAKE: Admiral, if I may. I had hoped to take out a ship and pursue the mutineers myself.

BAILEY: We feel that after the rigours of your last voyage, it would be prudent to assign you to a less demanding position. As for the mutineers, a ship was despatched to Capella 3 but found no sign of them. We have assumed that they headed into deep space in search of a new home. Given that our efforts in finding habitable planets in that sector have proven fruitless, we believe that they will have been unsuccessful. We ourselves have abandoned our search for habitable planets in that sector and moved our efforts to sector B6. Sending ships in search of the Endeavour has been dismissed as financially unviable. We believe that the mutineers will have died in space. May God have mercy on them.

FX: THE BELL AGAIN RINGS THREE TIMES.

SCENE 55. BURTON'S PLANET.

FLOWER: Well, John. What do you think?

FLETCHER: Not bad. Not bad at all, Doc.

ELENA: Not bad? It's easy seeing you didn't do the hard work.

FX: GURGLINGS OF A BABY.

ELENA: Say hello to your daughter.

FLETCHER: Hi. How does it feel to be the first person born on this planet?

ELENA: Hopefully better than it feels to have been the first person to give birth on the planet.

FLOWER: They've stopped work down in the village to get a celebration ready. Any excuse for a party really. Do you have a name picked.

FLETCHER: Yes. It's corny, but – we thought Hope.

ELENA: Hope.

FX: BABY GURGLES.

Notes

Okay, the first thing about *The Point of No Return* is that it hasn't actually been rejected. It's going to be produced sometime in the next few years from the time of writing this in March 2016. For me, this became a very interesting and ultimately led me to rework aspects of the script. What you hear on the radio when it gets produced will not be this precise version of the script.

Reading the script I realized there were some problems. First, some background on the script.

When I was younger, I saw Charles Laughton in *Mutiny on the Bounty*. The film really stuck with me. The 1962 remake less so, but the 1984 film *The Bounty* was also excellent and what took me with that was Anthony Hopkins' turn as Bligh. He didn't copy Laughton or Trevor Howard. Instead he built an interesting, layered character. That performance stayed with me, too. I was watching *Red River*, one of John Wayne's best westerns, and in its own way a retelling of the Mutiny on the Bounty, and I started to wonder about other ways to tell the story. As someone with a love of science fiction, for me, the obvious decision was space. So, why would they be in space? What would their mission be and how would that lead the Bligh and Fletcher Christian characters into conflict? It had to matter. It had to be important and it had to also be personal enough to give us character development. Earth's population growth was a big news story at the time. That filled the plot for me. Earth was crowded and couldn't feed everyone. Humanity needed a planet to colonise. Not Mars or the Moon where conditions and low gravity were hostile enemies, but an Earth-like world on which humanity could stretch and grow in recognizable conditions. So, if it was urgent for humanity to move, maybe Bligh had a family ho would suffer badly if a new world wasn't found… that would give him his motivation. That gave me the basis for the story.

This was the point where I picked names for the lead characters. I didn't want to use Bligh and Fletcher Christian so I chose similar names. John Fletcher for Fletcher Christian and for William Bligh… the name Blake kept coming to mind. I thought it was probably because I was a fan of Blake's 7, and so I ran other names through my head. I kept coming back to Blake, so there we had it – Blake and Fletcher.

If I had Blake's story worked out, I needed to do the name for Fletcher. One of the part of The Bounty that I liked most was that Bligh and Christian had been friends early in the piece. That made the breakdown of the relationship more potent when it happened. So, I gave Blake and Fletcher a strong relationship with Fletcher owing his position to Blake. They were friends on a first name basis. Fletcher Christian's relationship with a local woman in Tahiti was a big part in the *Bounty*'s story, so I needed a romantic interest for Fletcher. A female crewmember would have been lame. There wasn't really an option for a local girl from an island… it had to be someone with a reason to be out in space. So who would be in space? Colonists. A colony ship seeking a new world… and there we have Elena.

From there on it was quite straightforward with the plot. Fletcher and Elena get close, Blake suffers setbacks and becomes isolated from the crew. That leads him to feel the pressure of his mission, and to believe that the crew are turning against him. In turn he becomes tyrannical and Fletcher tries to ignore it and stay loyal to his captain until he is forced to make a decision between loyalty to his captain and loyalty to decency and the crew. It's pretty much the well-known story of the *Bounty*. The remainder of the crew were as multi-national as I could make it. I also decided to make the spaceship as naval as I possibly could. I've always thought spaceships would be like submarines – enclosed and claustrophobic with resources like air and fresh water at a premium. That was the atmosphere I wanted on the *Endeavour*. As soon as I started working the endeavor as a naval vessel, Captain Blake evolved into a future iteration of a Cornish seaman.

The script that is reprinted here is, roughly, forty five minute long. The original draft was aimed at a ninety minute slot, and obviously read much longer – roughly twice as many pages. They visited an extra planet, there were extra moments of breakdown of trust between Blake and the crew, and we saw the deaths of crew which opened up the position for Fletcher's promotion. The problem was that there was a lot going on, but it read as padding. It felt like sixty or sixty five minutes of plot expanded to ninety minutes. Looking at it, I chose to cut, rather than try to shore it up. I just didn't think it had enough plot for ninety minutes of radio. Oddly, I think it would have worked fine as ninety minutes of TV, but not radio.

The first draft of the script was very linear. When I got into the cutting, I knew that wouldn't work. I needed to get across some information that had been in the cut scenes. I didn't want to use a narrator. I've always thought narrators in radio drama are a bit of a cheat. Unless it's a piece of Victoriana, in which case the first person narrative is so rooted in that era's literature it's almost a pre-requisite and rude not to have one. Instead, I decided to have a narrative that started when the mutiny had already happened and then tell the story in extended flashbacks. I think it works pretty well. It allows me to get a lot of information into the plot quickly and to have a dynamic atmosphere straight from the start. I'm pretty pleased with the overall structure of this version.

But I'm not pleased with *everything*.

Blake's descent into mania is too quick in the script. For me, it feels like there is no moment when it begins. Now, in the real world, there would probably be no way to know the exact moment when it would begin, but this is a drama and I think we need to have a moment when the slow swing into paranoia begins. It may be something as simple as a small glitch in the ship that slows them down and he gets irritable and mutters that the mission is cursed. It won't be that because that is awful, but it could be something as minor as that. That gives us a moment to work from rather than just jumping straight into the developing mania.

The romance between Fletcher and Elena works quite nicely. I still like the guitar scene on the *Quatermain*. Again, though, I seem to have presented it as a *fait accomplis* that they were involved in a relationship. The relationship needs a little bit more at the start, just to give it a stronger base.

There are other things I would like to change. O'Leary will be changing nationality. The drunken Irishman, like the drunken Scotsman, is a stereotype and I'm not keen to further those stereotypes. Whichever nationality he winds up being, it's going to offend somebody and to whoever I do offend, I apologise.

One of the things I actually like about the cuts from ninety minutes to forty five minutes is that this is a story about people. I love science fiction. I always have. However, a lot of sci-fi falls into the trap of being about an event, a thing happening or a concept, and the characters in the story don't matter. Good sci-fi has a great central concept and characters the audience can relate to or would want to know better. The *Alien* films wouldn't have worked so well without Ripley there as the audience's anchor. There have been a lot of time travel shows, books and films, but

Doctor Who stays the course of time because we love that central character. The *TARDIS* is brilliant, the Daleks and Cybermen are iconic, the music is legendary… but the Doctor is a great character. No matter what kind of drama you're writing, be it family, historical, adventure, science fiction… whatever you're writing, you can't get anywhere without interesting characters. Always focus on your characters. In this piece, I do like Blake and Fletcher. I think Elena is strong, too. I'm a big believer in giving characters little details. It might be something as minor as, say, a woman wearing her dead mother's wedding ring on a chain around her neck. That means that she had a close relationship with her mother and misses her a lot. It pulls the audience in, makes them like the woman. It can be a habit, a trait, a hobby… maybe a bit of detail on a relationship or a memory that has affected them and their choices in life… just give the characters a little bit of something extra. When you're writing for radio, film or TV, those little extras are something for the performers to really get their teeth into.

THE LAST CHANCE

A half hour drama written for American radio.

FX: MOANING OF A MAN (WILL) WAKING FROM SLEEP.

CLAUDIA: (ON EDGE. SHAKEN)
             Wake up. Wake up!

WILL: (VERY SLEEPY, BEFUDDLED)
             What? Stop shouting. Who are you, anyway?
             Where are we? What is this place?

CLAUDIA: I don't know.

WILL: What do you mean you don't know?

CLAUDIA: I mean I don't know! Did you bring me here?

WILL: I don't even know where here is. It looks like
             somebody's apartment.

CLAUDIA: Well it's not mine.

WILL: Good. The decoration sucks.

CLAUDIA: There's something odd about this place.

WILL: What?

CLAUDIA: Look out of the window.

WILL: Okay. Which window where?

CLAUDIA: Exactly. I woke up about half an hour ago and
             I've looked around the apartment. It has a
             bedroom, a bathroom, this place, another small
             room that's set up as an office. But none of the
             rooms have a window.

WILL: That doesn't make sense. Nobody with a brain
             would build a home without any windows. Would
             they?

CLAUDIA: So maybe it wasn't built by someone in their right mind.

WILL: What are you talking about… what's your name?

CLAUDIA: Claudia Gianni.

WILL: Will Thorpe. What were you saying?

CLAUDIA: What's the last thing you remember before waking up here?

WILL: I'm not sure. My head's fuzzy. It feels like somebody's wrapped my brain in wet cotton wool.

CLAUDIA: That'll pass in a few minutes. Try to remember. Where were you?

WILL: St Barts. I'm a doctor in paediatrics there. I'd pulled a long stretch. One of the kids I was treating took a turn for the bad so I stayed late. Missed what looked like a pretty good New Years party for it. She picked up around three in the morning so I decided to drive home.

FX: FOOTSTEPS FADE IN AS HIS RECAP FADES INTO BEING THE NARRATIVE.

WILL: (VO)
             I was half asleep. I didn't hear anyone come close to me in the car park.

MAN: Doctor Thorpe?

WILL: Yeah? What…

FX: SOUNDS OF A STRUGGLE AND A YELL FROM WILL THEN THE FLASHBACK FADES OUT.

ON THE SHELF

WILL: There were three or four of them. All dressed in
               black. I only caught sight of them for a moment
               then I felt something sharp at my neck.

FX: HAND SNAPPING TO NECK.

CLAUDIA: It was an injection. I got one too. See?

FX: NECK OF CLOTHING PULLED A LITTLE.

WILL: Must have been a fast acting sedative. Nembutol
               maybe. How did you get here?

CLAUDIA: Pretty much the same as you. For New Years I
               went out with some friends from work - I teach at
               the Roosevelt. I was designated driver. I dropped
               my friends off - they were creamed. One of my
               tyres blew out so I pulled over. I was checking the
               tyre when I felt he sting in my neck.
               (BEAT, THEN WRY HUMOUR)
               What do you think this is? Some whacko serial
               killer?

WILL: They're usually loners but it was a bunch of guys
               that grabbed me.

CLAUDIA: A cult then?

WILL: I don't know. You don't have any friends who
               like practical jokes, do you?

CLAUDIA: Some joke.

FX: WILL STANDING.

CLAUDIA: You needn't bother with the door. I tried. It's
               locked.

FX: RATTLE OF DOOR HANDLE.

79

WILL:	No harm in trying. There must be a way out of here.
CLAUDIA:	There isn't. I looked.
WILL:	No harm in me having another look.
CLAUDIA:	Wait.
WILL:	What?
CLAUDIA:	Nothing. I just don't want to be on my own, that's all. But I don't know if…
WILL:	If you can trust me. How do I know I can trust you?
CLAUDIA:	You don't.
WILL:	Brilliant. Does that TV work?
CLAUDIA:	Try it.

FX: CLICK THEN NOTHING.

WILL:	Old glory?
CLAUDIA:	It's on all of the channels.
WILL:	All? There are only three. This is crazy. Have you looked in all the rooms?
CLAUDIA:	I think so but… I feel stupid saying it.
WILL	What?
CLAUDIA:	I didn't want to be on my own so I didn't stay in them long.
WILL:	Show me the rooms. Please.

FX: FOOTSTEPS, DOOR.

CLAUDIA: The kitchen.

WILL: With a dining table? Cosy.

CLAUDIA: The bathroom's along here.

FX: LIGHT CLICKS ON.

WILL: A shower and a bath? Somebody likes their
              comforts.

CLAUDIA: There's a little office over there.

FX: DOOR OPENS, LIGHT ON.

WILL: Weird.

CLAUDIA: All this and you find the office weird?

WILL: Yeah. No. Sorry. It's just that… well, it's sort of
              like my office at home. The way the shelves are
              set. What else?

CLAUDIA: There's another room next to this one. It's
              smaller. And… see for yourself.

FX: DOOR OPENS. LIGHT.

WILL: A nursery? Never used by the look of things.

FX: JINGLE OF A MOBILE.

CLAUDIA: That leads from through into a bedroom.

FX: DOOR OPENS.

CLAUDIA: But who'd have a nursery with no windows?

WILL: Same people who'd have a whole house with no windows.

FX: DOOR SLIDES OPEN.

CLAUDIA: Look at this.

WILL: What?

FX: RATTLE OF CLOTHES HANGERS.

WILL: Clothes. Wait a damn minute. Those are my clothes. Well, some of them. That jacket.

CLAUDIA: Those dresses are mine. And the overcoat.

WILL: Try the drawers.

FX: DRAWER PULLED OUT.

WILL: Recognise any of this?

CLAUDIA: All of it. That's my underwear!

FX: DRAWERS PULLED OUT.

CLAUDIA: My t-shirts, blouses.

WILL: The bottom two are full of my clothes. Jeans, boxers, shorts, the lot.

FX: CUPBOARD DOOR OPENS. CARDBOARD BOX OPENED.

CLAUDIA: These boxes in the cupboards. They've been in my apartment. Pictures, CDs… These are my things.

WILL: This one's got my stuff in it. They've emptied my office by the looks of it. What the hell's going on here?

FX: A SLIGHT FANFARE IN THE DISTANCE.

CLAUDIA: The TV.

FX: DOOR OPENS. THEY RUN THROUGH. TV IS NOW
PLAYING. CHARLES DOHERTY IS ON THE SCREEN,
SPEAKING.

DOHERTY: By now you will be wondering what has
             happened to you. I will explain.

CLAUDIA: (QUIETLY, OVER DOHERTY)
             That's Charles Doherty. He's a senator. I thought
             he died last year.

WILL: Quiet. I want to hear.

DOHERTY: My friends, there's no easy way to say this, so
             straight talk is probably the best. Four years ago,
             astronomers discovered that a group of asteroids
             were on a trajectory that would bring them into
             the path of the Earth. The data was analysed,
             checked and rechecked. But there was no mistake.
             Earth would be hit. If you remember the impact
             the Schumacher-Levy comet had on Jupiter some
             years ago, well, that's what we expect to happen
             to Earth. A rain of smaller fragments – small by
             cosmic standards but enough to cause plenty of
             damage by themselves. But then we think there
             will be three much bigger impacts. We can't
             predict exactly how much damage these will do -
             but our best guess is the equivalent of a hundred
             year nuclear winter. Governments conferred in
             secret and decided on the best course of action.
             We can't stop the asteroids and we can't save
             everyone on the planet. But we can save the
             human race. There are hundreds, thousands of
             bunkers three kilometres deep underground all
             across the world, each has a thousand people in it.
             Doctors, engineers, scientists, poets, teachers,
             artists… we've saved the people we need to

Iain McLaughlin

rebuild the world. That's you. You are in one of these bunkers. You were picked because our scan of medical records showed you were strong and healthy and genetically right for this task.
(BEAT)
There are two of you in each room, watching this. Get to know the person you're with. That is your husband or that is your wife. Most of you had loved ones, husbands, wives, fiances… forget them. Forget them. This is your life now. These are desperate times and you are our last, our only hope. The first of the asteroids will be coming down today. God help us all.

FIRST COMMERCIAL

FX: TV SWITCHED OFF.

CLAUDIA: What are you doing? I want to…

WILL: I've seen enough. Do you believe it? What he said?

CLAUDIA: I don't know. Do you?

WILL: I… maybe. Why would anyone go to all this trouble if it wasn't?

CLAUDIA: Nobody knew anything about the asteroids. There was nothing on the news.

WILL: I didn't think anyone could keep a secret anymore – not with the internet and cell phones.

CLAUDIA: Cell phone.

FX: A PURSE BEING RIFLED THROUGH.

CLAUDIA: We can phone people. Warn them about the asteroids.

84

ON THE SHELF

FX: NUMBERS PUNCHED INTO THE PHONE.

CLAUDIA: Come on, damn it.

WILL: If we're three kilometres underground, there's no
             way you'll get a signal out.

CLAUDIA: But I have family. My mom, my grandma,
             sisters…

WILL: Maybe they've been lucky and been picked for
             other shelters.

CLAUDIA: My sisters, maybe but not the others. You heard
             him. You saw the nursery. You know what we're
             here for. Breeding. Like cattle.

WILL: Do you have someone? Husband? Boyfriend?

CLAUDIA: Yeah. No. Not really. It hasn't been going
             anywhere for a while. I think we'd split up but
             hadn't mentioned it to each other yet. You?

WILL: Kind of. It's a bit of a cliché. Grace Verdi. She's
             a nurse.

CLAUDIA: I see what you mean about cliché. Doctor and
             nurse.

WILL: She wanted to keep it simple with us. She didn't
             want to get heavy with someone she worked with.

CLAUDIA: Smart girl.

WILL: Smart, sexy, funny. The hospital's going to be
             over-run when the asteroids come down.

CLAUDIA: If it survives. If anything survives.

WILL: I should be there. I'm a doctor. I should be there.

FX: A MUFFLED IMPACT. DISTANT BUT CLEARLY A
LARGE, POWERFUL IMPACT.

CLAUDIA: It's too late.

WILL: It's started.

FX: TV CLICKS ON.

CLAUDIA: What are you doing?

WILL: I need to see it.

CLAUDIA: I don't. I don't need to see my family die.

FX: FOOTSTEPS HURRYING. DOOR CLOSING.

DOHERTY: (ON TV)
                I'd advise you all to switch your sets off and take
                this time for prayer. But for those of you who
                need to see this, we have access to NASA
                satellites and international intelligence to keep
                track of what's happening above. The United
                States has been hit by two small asteroids so far,
                one of them close by our position. A heavier
                barrage is due in a few hours. The prediction is
                that the Earth's rotation will bring the
                Mediterranean into the firing line of these.

FX: SMALL BUZZ ON TV.

DOHERTY: That's another impact on the United States.
                Wyoming. Two more are coming in. One will hit
                near Austin in Texas, the other just north of
                Baltimore.

WILL: (QUIETLY)
                It's the end of the world.

MUSIC: SOMBRE BRIDGE.

FX: DOOR OPENS.

WILL: Oh.

CLAUDIA: (VOICE CHOKED, UPSET)
               I'm not asleep. How bad is it?

WILL: Bad. More than thirty asteroids hit the States.
               That's not quite right. Some of them detonated in
               the atmosphere. Apparently that's worse.

CLAUDIA: It's over?

WILL: No. This is just the warm-up. The real big ones
               arrive tomorrow and the day after.

CLAUDIA: What's it like? On the surface? Have you heard?

WILL: We caught some TV reports before they blacked
               out. Some places have rioting, looting. Some
               places aren't affected by it and they're going
               about their business like any other day. And some
               people are banding together, helping the injured,
               looking after the old. The hospitals can't cope but
               good people are finding a way.

CLAUDIA: What about Minnesota? My mom's on vacation
               there?

WILL: I don't remember hearing anything about
               Minnesota taking a hit.

CLAUDIA: Thank god.

WILL: Chicago wasn't so lucky. My mother and her
               husband live there.

CLAUDIA: I'm sorry.

WILL: He was a good guy. He made Mom feel alive
               again after Dad died. She won't have been alone.

CLAUDIA: She might have survived. You never know.

WILL: (NOT BUYING IT FOR A MOMENT)
             Maybe. There's something else. They've
             unlocked our doors. Well, released the locks to
             our control. Our key number is 6-5-6-1.

CLAUDIA: 6-5-6-1.

WILL: I don't want to see anyone. But I don't want to
             stay here either.

CLAUDIA: I'd rather see people. I need to see other people.
             Just to know there are some.

WILL: Okay.

FX: QUIET RUMBLE OF PEOPLE. A SLIGHT ECHO TO
SHOW THEY'RE INSIDE.

CLAUDIA: I don't know what I was expecting but it wasn't
             this. There are some families here. Kids.

WILL: I thought it would be more like a bomb shelter.
             This reminds me of a hotel I stayed at for a
             conference once.

CLAUDIA: Everybody's going this way.

WILL: It's as good a way as any.

ALAN: Did you watch the report?

CLAUDIA: No. Will - my… friend - did.

WILL: Yeah.

ALAN: The woman in my room - my wife they'd call her.
             She wanted to know about New York. That's
             where her family is.

WILL: They didn't mention New York. Looks like it
            didn't take a hit this time.

ALAN: That's a relief. Thanks.

WILL: At least somebody gets good news today. I'm
            Will Thorpe.

ALAN: Alan Wise. I probably should go back to... I
            don't even know her name... I don't know
            anything.

FX: ALAN'S FOOTSTEPS MOVE OFF.

WILL: This must be the central point of the complex.
            That looks like a notice board - and a map.

CLAUDIA: How can this work? They can't throw people
            together and hope they make couples.

DOHERTY: That's exactly what we're doing, Claudia. May I
            call you Claudia? Oh, I'm sorry. I didn't mean to
            startle you.

ALAN: We didn't hear you coming across.

CLAUDIA: You move pretty well for a dead man.

DOHERTY: You're only the second person who's recognised
            me. I think the party was right when they said I
            wasn't memorable enough to run for President.

ALAN: So why the deception? The disappearance?

DOHERTY: To oversee the building of these shelters and the
            selection process.

CLAUDIA: You selected us? You son of...

DOHERTY: The computer selected you and paired you.
            You're both exactly what the human race needs

in the future. Oh, I know you both. I've studied everybody's files. We'll need a doctor like never before. Not just to treat patients but to help train new doctors. And you, Claudia. We have families here. Children are our future. We need teachers for them.

CLAUDIA: And parents to breed them.

DOHERTY: That's not quite how I'd have phrased it but I'm afraid, yes. However important your jobs are in the shelter, your most vital task is to make babies.

WILL: And if we don't get on? Say we hate each other?

DOHERTY: You won't. The computers are sure you'll get along just fine.

WILL: Then let the computers make the babies.

DOHERTY: They can do many things but that, thankfully, is left to us humans. If you'll excuse me, I have to go and see the farmers. We have a little farm down here – enough for fresh milk, eggs, meat - we even grow some crops. Or we will if we can get the farmers to tend them quickly enough. I'll talk to you again soon.
(BEAT)
You two will do fine together.

WILL: Want a bet?

FX: DOHERTY'S FOOTSTEPS HEADING AWAY.

WILL: Looks, if that sounded like I was insulting you, Claudia…

CLAUDIA: It's okay. I understand. This isn't exactly what I'd planned for my wedding day either.

WILL: Wedding day? I hadn't thought of it like that. I should feel something about that. Angry, maybe. At being lied to, at being brought here against my will, at being forced to stay here when I should be out there helping people.

CLAUDIA: What do you feel?

WILL: Nothing. Just numb. Like I'm on autopilot.

CLAUDIA: I know. I should mourn my family but I don't know if they're dead - or if they'll die tomorrow. Or next week or next month when there's no food for them. I… I don't know what to do. What I should feel.

WILL: Everybody is the same. Look at them. They're not really talking to each other. They just want to be with people.

CLAUDIA: I don't know if I can face being with people.

WILL: You could go back to…

CLAUDIA: But I know I can't face being there alone.

FX: DISTANT RUMBLE OF AN IMPACT. CROWD RESPONDS WITH FEAR AND ALARM.

WILL: This deep we should be able to survive anything short of a direct hit.

CLAUDIA: What will we survive as? Strangers forced to cower underground and breed like cattle while their families die up on the surface? If we do that, are we worth saving?

WILL: This wasn't our choice. I don't see any way out – and believe me, I'd rather be up there trying to help people. But none of us has any choice in this. We have to get by somehow.

CLAUDIA: Make the best of it?

WILL: That's not how I would have put it but in
             essence... what choice do we have?

CLAUDIA: (MISERABLE)
             It won't work. It can't. People can't just live lives
             down here as if nothing's happened up above?
             How can kids come to a school knowing their
             friends, most of their families, are dead?

WILL: I don't know. If this place last a week I'll be
             surprised. People can't just be paired off like this.

CLAUDIA: It just won't work.

SECOND COMMERCIAL

FX: JINGLE OF LITTLE BELLS. CHRISTMAS MUSIC PLAYS.
DOOR OPENS.

WILL: Hi, hon. Sorry. I promised to stop calling you
             'hon' in class, didn't I?

CLAUDIA: It's okay. None of the kids are here.

FX: BELLS JINGLE LOUDER.

WILL: What's this?

CLAUDIA: A sleigh. The kids made it for me as a Christmas
             present.

WILL: Unbelievable. Even after the longest part of a year
             down here, people are clinging to their traditions.
             I can't believe we're having Christmas holidays.
             Except for your small town doc here, who's on
             call and convinced Maria Jennings will start her
             labour as soon as he sits down to Christmas
             dinner.

CLAUDIA: If she does, there'll be trouble. Still, she'll be glad to get it over with. She's huge - and tired all the time.

WILL: She hasn't been scaring you with stories of her horror pregnancy, has she?

CLAUDIA: I'm only two months pregnant. I've got all of that in front of me.

WILL: And you're still beautiful. Anyway, rather than have this discussion again, you could tell me why you brought me here.

CLAUDIA: It's kind of dumb.

WILL: So am I. Shoot.

CLAUDIA: Did you have a computer glitch this afternoon?

WILL: Yeah. A small one but it didn't do any major damage. Why?

CLAUDIA: It seems to have reset something in my computer. Normally I can only access the educational database.

WILL: And now?

CLAUDIA: I can see an awful lot more. I had a little look through the system. Look at these. Security cameras in the lower storage chambers.

WILL: Great. You can look at ten years of food supplies.

FX: KEY PRESSED.

CLAUDIA: Look at this one.

WILL: What am I looking... wait up. Is that an elevator?

CLAUDIA: Keep watching. I've been watching for almost an hour and it's been making trips up and down constantly. Here it is.

WILL: That's damn peculiar. It looks like they're re-stocking our provisions.

CLAUDIA: That's exactly what they're doing.

WILL: But how? They said there's no food on the surface.

CLAUDIA: There's only one way to find out what's going on.

MUSIC: BRIDGE.

FX: KEYPAD PUNCHED. DOOR OPENS.

CLAUDIA: I saw one of the guards punch in the pass number.

WILL: Now you tell me about the guards.

FX: DOOR CLOSES. SOUND OF MOVING VEHICLES.

CLAUDIA: (QUIETLY)
If we stay in the shadows we should be able to avoid the guards and the cameras.

FX: QUIET FOOTSTEPS.

WILL: If we get caught in here we'll be in real trouble.

CLAUDIA: The we don't get caught. Look. There's one of the transport wagons.

WILL: It's empty. Keep an eye out. I'm going for a look-see.

FX: SCUTTLING FOOTSTEPS. FLIP OF TARPAULIN.

WILL: Nothing.

FX: CAB DOOR OPENS.

CLAUDIA: Found anything?

WILL: I told you to keep an eye out.

CLAUDIA: You'd abandon your pregnant wife? Is there anything in here?

WILL: Not that I... wait.

FX: NEWSPAPER GRABBED.

WILL: A newspaper. That's today's date.

CLAUDIA: They've still got newspapers? They must be recovering quicker than we expected.

WILL: I don't understand it. Look. There's nothing about the asteroids in the paper. It's all about Christmas, the holidays. Travel early, get to the airport in plenty of time, buy last minute presents...

CLAUDIA: They can't have rebuilt things so fast. The papers should be full of how they're dealing with the asteroid damage.

WILL: The weather report - they're saying it's the mildest winter in years. It should be a nuclear winter. I don't understand.

CLAUDIA: I want to see what it's like on the surface. Help me into the back of the wagon.

WILL: What? Claudia...

CLAUDIA: And hurry. We can't have long before the driver comes back.

FX: RATTLE OF ELEVATOR. GATE-DOORS CLANK OPEN.

DRIVER: Here's my pass.

GUARD: Any more runs? We need to close this place up.

DRIVER: One more - but I need a bathroom break first.

GUARD: Hurry it up.

FX: TRUCK TRUNDLES ON THEN COMES TO A STOP. CAB DOOR OPENS AND CLOSES.

WILL: He's gone.

CLAUDIA: Where are we?

WILL: Looks like a cave. Or a mine that's been broadened out to take these wagons.

CLAUDIA: They were talking about closing us up.

WILL: I heard. The cave exit should be… this way.

FX: FOOTSTEPS ON SANDY GROUND.

CLAUDIA: There. There's light.

WILL: Keep moving.

CLAUDIA: It's daylight. Sunlight.

GUARD 2:   Hey. Who are you? What are you doing in…

FX: A SOLID THUMP. GUARD 2 FALLS.

WILL: I probably shouldn't have done that.

CLAUDIA: Come on. We're almost there.

FX: MORE FOOTSTEPS. SOUND OF BREEZE THROUGH TREES.

WILL: We're out. It's…

CLAUDIA: It's a sham. Everything that's happened over the past year. There weren't any asteroids. No asteroids, no nuclear winter. Nothing. It's a sham. A fake.

WILL: I don't understand. Why?

CLAUDIA: We need to get away from here. Contact the press. I have to contact my mother.

DOHERTY: Claudia! Will! What are you doing out here?

FX: FOOTSTEPS RUNNING TOWARDS THEM.

CLAUDIA: Why did you lie? Why have you had us living like rats underground? There haven't been any asteroids or meteors. What is this? Some stupid experiment? Are we lab rats for you?

DOHERTY: It's not like that, Claudia. Come back inside the shelter, please. We don't have much time.

WILL: You don't have any time. We're going to the press with this. We're going to TV. We'll tell them everything.

DOHERTY: The press aren't going to care. They have the asteroids to worry about.

WILL: There aren't any asteroids!

DOHERTY: Not yet. Listen to me. Most of what you've been told is true. There are asteroids and there are hundreds of shelters all over the world to help humanity survive. Only the time was changed. We needed to know if this would all work, so we brought you down a year before the asteroids would hit. It was so that we could work out any problems and have everything running smoothly

> before the asteroids came. We even used the detonations from the expansion of the mine network here to simulate an asteroid impact nearby.

CLAUDIA: I don't believe you.

DOHERTY: It's true. Now please. Go back into the shelter. Oh, no. It's starting.

WILL: What?

FX: SOUND OF AN ASTEROID HISSING THROUGH THE SKY. A DISTANT EXPLOSION AS IT HITS.

DOHERTY: The first wave of smaller asteroids. Hundreds of them. There's another.

FX:ANOTHER ASTEROID HISSING ACROSS THE SKY.

WILL: There's another one.

DOHERTY: I'm going into the shelter. If you choose to stay out here that's your decision. The shutters will close in two minutes.

FX: FEET RUN FOR THE MINE ENTRANCE. ASTEROIDS ZING ACROSS THE SKY.

CLAUDIA: No!

WILL: We can't stay here. We have to go back inside.

CLAUDIA: We can't go through this again. All the people we love…

WILL: They died a year ago! This never happened. We were never up here.

CLAUDIA: But…

WILL: No buts! We can't do anything for them. The only person we can save is our baby. We have to go back inside. Now! Come on!

FX: FEET ON SAND AS METAL DOORS BEGIN TO GRIND SHUT.

WILL: We're coming in. Hold the gates.

FX: MORE FOOTSTEPS.

WILL: Okay.

DOHERTY: Seal the outer shutters and prime secondary shutters. You did the right thing coming back inside. You...

FX: A HARD, VICIOUS SLAP.

CLAUDIA: Don't talk to me. Don't ever talk to me.

DOHERTY: Will, if the others in the shelter find out, there could be chaos.

WILL: We won't tell them - for their sake not yours. Today never happened. Do you understand?

DOHERTY: Yes.

CLAUDIA: Will, let's get away from here.

WILL: Come on. Let's go home. The only home we have left.

FX: SOUND OF THE ELEVATOR AND THE DISTANT SOUND OF A METEOR IMPACT.

Notes

Claire Bartlett and I wrote this for Imagination Theatre but somehow it just never seems to have found a slot in their schedules. It was written in the style of a Twilight Zone. Being honest, I was very tempted to put in a bit of Twilight Zone-ish narration, but that would have taken things too far onto their patch. I like to homage and give a nod to other people's work. The narration would have been just too much.

The story came out of seeing a bunch of meteor disaster movies – *Armageddon*, *Deep Impact* and the wonderfully cast but appallingly dull *Meteor*. I was interested in how countries would try to survive. When we started plotting we originally included scenes of Will and Claudia being drugged and captured. The idea was to start with a bit of action and then move into a mystery and a bit of exposition. However, once we got into writing, that little opening sequence really threw the pacing and rhythm of the episode off. We talked about it and decided to start with the mystery. I liked that much better. It asked questions and felt more organic than a pair of bolted on kidnap scenes. Cropping those kidnap scenes also did something really important – it removed characters. It will be mentioned again later in this book, but when you write for audio and radio, you have to be aware of the size of cast you're liable to have, and how many characters you can use. Actors often double up playing one character at the start of a play and another at the end. They do the same on stage. When they're on stage they use costumes, wigs and make-up to disguise that it's the same actor. On radio it's about disguising the voices. So, I generally give these smaller roles accents so push the actors in various directions with their performances. However, it's worth pointing out that some actors can struggle with accents, and every now and then you do get moments in which you wonder what the hell is going on. Ninety nine times out of a hundred, though, your director will get a perfectly acceptable accent and you won't notice it.

I am, actually, very fond of this little play. It was a very deliberate change of pace, to write it with the feel of *The Twilight Zone*, and also to try to make it a bit more Old Time Radio than we normally write. I think it works pretty well. If I was to make changes, there are things I would definitely do. I would give us more time of Will and Claudia together in the year underground. We jump from them meeting to a year later when they have accepted that this is their lot and they are having a baby together. I would have given them a bit of time together, to at least indicate some time when they bond between them started to grow. We deliberately didn't put that in for this iteration of the play, choosing to jump forward a year. I think it works as it is but that it would work better if we had a bit of time developing their characters. I'd also like to develop the sense of community that's developed underground. Doherty mentions at the end that they will hurt people if they reveal the truth. I think that if we show more of the community and friendships that have developed, that would have much more impact. It doesn't take a lot to grow that community. It only needs to be a line or two about meeting friends or choosing to spend time with others in a social area. You can get a lot of information into a short piece of dialogue and on radio that is a great thing if you can do it well.

Incidentally, the characters' names, Will and Claudia... *Carry On* fans might just remember a woman named Willa Claudia from *Carry On Cleo*. Yep., that's where the name comes from. Naming characters isn't easy. The names have to *feel* right. The names have to feel like they belong on those characters, like they can live their lives wearing those names. I occasionally struggle with names, so I run through the names of football teams, authors, the music charts of a particular week until I find names that feel right for all the characters. If you check the names of the supporting characters of *The Wasting*, a play Claire and I wrote for Big Finish's *UNIT* series you'll find the surnames of all the *James Bond* novel authors and members of Dundee United's league winning team of the 1982-83 season. Everybody finds their own way to choose names but those are a decent way to start.

A Stitch in Time

A four part *Doctor Who* adventure submitted to Big Finish Productions in Spring 2000 for their licensed series of audio plays. It was rejected in Autumn 2000.

Episode 1

1.

St Peter's Memorial Hospital. New York. Day.
It's getting near Christmas. We can hear carol singing in the distance. Dr Alan Rigg (he's 30-ish) is making his weary way through the corridor. There's a drunken belch from a patient.

ALAN: Woah. Careful there, Santa. Toomuch festive cheer at the office party? No, I guess not. Nasty. ER's back that way.

Drunken belch of gratitude.

ALAN: Who'd do a thing like that to Santa? I guess whoever it is isn't getting any presents this year.

Door opening. Alan yawns mightily.

ALAN: I should have asked Santa for twelve hours' sleep.

He's disturbed by a tinny voice on the tannoy.

VOICE: Dr Alan Rigg to the Ward 12. Dr Alan Rigg to Ward 12.

ALAN: I guess I'm not getting it. That's the last time I'm nice to Santa.

2.

US Military Research Base, New York State. Day.
The Base's CO, General John Broxton is in a room buzzing with energy and low conversation. Broxton is maybe mid-forties; young for a general but strong and vibrant.

BROXTON: Gentlemen, are we ready to begin?

Iain McLaughlin

SCIENTIST: Well, General, a few more days...

BROXTON: A few more days will lead to a few more after
                 that. We've had enough delays on this
                 project. The Pentagon is breathing down my
                 neck. They want something in return for the
                 billions of tax-dollars they've ploughed into
                 this enterprise. And more important, my wife
                 claims that this project has got me acting
                 cranky. Now, I could deal with having to tell
                 Washington that we need more time for tests
                 but I don't think I can take another lecture
                 from my wife. Let's give ourselves the best
                 Christmas present we can - and get a positive
                 result for the project. Any objections?

No answer.

BROXTON: That's what I wanted to hear. Let's get this
                 under way.

3.
The hospital.
Alan is yawning. He's approached by a nurse.

NURSE: Alan? What are you doing here? I thought
                 you were off duty three hours ago.

ALAN: You know Kelly? The nurse in pediatrics?
                 With the big... hair.

NURSE: You and her?

ALAN: Her and Jon Blake. I'm covering for him.

NURSE: Again? And I bet you're working Christmas
                 Day again as well. You spend your time
                 saving lives - maybe you should think about
                 getting on with living one as well.

ALAN: I'm glad you're a good nurse, coz you're a
               rotten psychiatrist.

A door slams.

ALAN: Jon? I thought you and Kelly...

BLAKE: (Not happy)
               She was on call. Go home.

ALAN: Sounds good to me. 'Bye, people.

4.
The Tardis. Interior.
The Sixth Doctor and Peri are in residence and aren't bickering.
Their relationship is steadier - more like the way it was in *The
Mysterious Planet*.

DOCTOR: New York? Peri, why on Earth do you want
               to go to New York? Especially in 1985. I
               mean, it's hardly a vintage year. Now I could
               take you back to see the American Indians
               sell the land to the Dutch, or how about a
               speakeasy during Prohibition?

PERI: No thanks, Doctor. 1985 will do fine.

DOCTOR: 1962? Bob Dylan in Greenwich Village,
               singing A Hard Rain's Gonna Fall during the
               Cuban Missile Crisis? 2112 to see the replica
               Titanic sail in to the harbour on her maiden
               voyage?

PERI: '85.

DOCTOR: Oh, all right. Though I don't see what's so
               special about New York in 1985. It's such a
               pedestrian year.

PERI: It's home.

DOCTOR: You want to go home? You're not thinking of leaving are you?

PERI: Would you miss me if I did decide to go?

DOCTOR: My dear Peri, I have traveled with numerous companions over a vast number of years. You're not the first and you won't be the last. (BEAT) And yes, I would miss you. Rather a lot.

PERI: Thanks. And relax, I don't want to leave you, but I would like to let my mother know I'm okay. Okay? I've been traveling with you for years now without ever visiting home. Mom would probably have worried herself grey by now - if she didn't have the bottle of dye in the medicine cabinet.

DOCTOR: All right. New York, 1985, it is.

5.
Military Research Centre.
The machinery is getting cranked up. Broxton is still overseeing things.

BROXTON: How long?

SCIENTIST: Everything's set... now, General.

BROXTON: Good. Hand me that recorder, would you? Thanks. December 23rd, 1985. Today, here at the Von Braun Research Facility in New York State, on behalf of the American Government, we are about to make history. Using strange matter to warp space and time, we intend to instantaneously transport an object from one sealed chamber, through a lead partition to another. If this experiment is successful, the technology has limitless potential for transporting people, food and other resources. The military potential should not be overlooked either. General John Broxton recording.

He switches the recorder off.

BROXTON: All recording devices on?

SCIENTIST: On.

BROXTON: Then saddle up. It's time we earned our pay. Begin primary power build-up.

The hum of the machinery gets louder.

SCIENTIST: Rising... fifty percent... seventy five... power levels at optimum.

BROXTON: Scan and matt the target block of lead.

SCIENTIST: Lead block being matted. Dimensions and composition logged in computer.

BROXTON: Begin transfer procedure.

SCIENTIST: Initiating warp bubble around target object. Bubble set and holding.
BROXTON: Transfer.

The machinery is louder and then glitches. The steady noise fritzes and crackles. Something is badly wrong.

BROXTON: What's wrong? Why hasn't the block transferred?

SCIENTIST: We're losing warp bubble integrity.

BROXTON: Hold it steady.

SCIENTIST: I'm trying, general. I'll try compensating by
              moving to a lower frequency bandwidth. It's
              not working. Integrity down to forty six
              percent. Twenty eight... fifteen... it's gone.

The sound of machinery has died. There is a moment of dead
calm - depressed failure.

BROXTON: What happened?

SCIENTIST: I don't know, General.

BROXTON: I want every single piece of data relating to
              this experiment analysed. If we find out what
              went wrong here, we can learn from our
              mistake - and this won't have been the total
              failure it looks like. If anything comes up, I'll
              be in my office, reporting to Washington.

Broxton closes a door behind him. We hear him pick up a
phone and punch a number.

BROXTON: Get me Chief-of-Staff Sheridan at the
              Pentagon.

A slight delay while the call is relayed.

BROXTON: Good to hear from you as well, sir. Not good,
              I'm afraid. Well, we're working on that.

There's a buzz from the intercom.

BROXTON: Would you excuse me for a minute, please.

Beep from the intercom.

BROXTON: What is it?

It's the scientist - and he's frantic.

SCIENTIST: The block of lead - it's emitting tachyon particles. We can't stop it. It's building a warp field and we can't shut it down. Oh, God, it's out of control. It's giving out types of radiation we've never seen before. I don't know what's happening here.

The sound from the warp bubble is building.

SCIENTIST: General, do something.

BROXTON: Get out of there. Get out of there now!

SCIENTIST: It's out of control. It's going to...

The scientist's scream is drowned by a strange, screeching explosion.

6.
New York.
Alan is driving home. There are honks of horns and the rumble of idling engines in a traffic jam.

ALAN: Come on. Come on. I'd like to get home before New Year's. God, I hate Christmas traffic.

Honk of horn.

ALAN: Yeah. And you, butt-munch. Why don't you ask Santa to bring you a brain this year, huh?

There is a rumbling, screeching sound - the one from the lab - only now it is wilder and getting louder. Horns honk and people begin screaming.

ALAN: Now what?

The sound - and the screams - get louder.

ALAN: What the hell...?

Screech of tyres as the sound gets louder. Honks his horn.

ALAN: Out of the way. Get out of the damn way.

Crash of glass as he smashes through a plate glass window. The sound gets louder until it overwhelms everything.

7.
New York.
The wind whistles as the TARDIS makes her customary, noisy materialisation. The doors open.

PERI: That was a bumpier landing than usual.

DOCTOR: Was it indeed? Nonetheless, as madam
               requested here we are in nineteen eighty...

He pauses a little as he obviously emerges, his feet scrunching in snow, a strong, arctic wind whistling.

DOCTOR: ...five?

The wind continues whistling. This is clearly a cold, wintry scene.

PERI: Good try. Doctor, but I'd guess a few
               thousand years out. We've landed in an ice
               age.

DOCTOR: This *is* 1985 - the TARDIS' instruments were quite clear about it.

PERI: If this is 1985, where have we landed, then? Greenland? Iceland? With glaciers like these it must be Antarctica.

DOCTOR: Do any of those places have street signs like this?

PERI: What? You're right. I can't make out what it says. The ice is too thick. Wait... something and   Broadway? Doctor, this is New York!

DOCTOR: So it would seem.

PERI: What happened? This can't be just a bad winter. This street sign isn't just covered with snow - it's encased in ice. It's solid.

DOCTOR: I'm not surprised. From the oxygen content and the compression, I'd say this ice is 30,000 years old, give or take a year or two either way. And yet according to the Tardis, this is New York, on December 23rd, 1985. I thought you might like to spend Christmas with your family.

PERI: What's happened here?

DOCTOR: I don't know - but I jolly well intend to find out.

PERI: Look, these aren't just glaciers. There are buildings stuck in the ice.

DOCTOR: Encased would be more accurate. Careful. Don't touch the ice. The moisture in your skin will freeze to it.

PERI: (Thoughtful)
                If this really is Broadway... I know exactly
                where we are.

DOCTOR: Before we go anywhere you should go and
                dress in something warmer - and bring my
                cloak while you're at it. Even I'm feeling the
                chill.

PERI: Okay.

DOCTOR: I think we're in for a cold day in New York
                City.

8.
New York.
In his crashed car, Alan is coming round. He groans.

ALAN: God, my head.

Sound of him shoving at the door and trying the handle.

ALAN: Hey. Somebody want to give me a hand here?
                Hey. Anybody?

No answer.

ALAN: Never mind. Tell you what. I'll get it myself.
                I'm only stuck in here, but that's okay.

The door finally creaks open with that screeching sound of
metal scraping against metal that's almost like fingernails on a
blackboard. His feet crunch on broken glass. The wind is
howling coldly outside.

ALAN: Where is everybody? Anybody here? Jeez.
                What the hell happened?

He moves through the glass, his feet scrunching it underfoot.

ALAN: Damn broken glass is a deathtrap.

Now he's outside, the wind is louder.

ALAN: Hello? Anybody hear me? Is anybody here?
                   Hello? Answer if you hear me! Hello?

No answer.

ALAN: Where the hell is everybody?

Still no answer; just the howling winds.

9.
New York.
The Doctor and Peri are walking through the snow, the wind
howling about them.

PERI: Okay, remind me whose idiot idea it was to
                   come to New York in 1985.

DOCTOR: But if you hadn't wanted to come here, we'd
                   never have found this little mystery, would
                   we?

PERI: You know, I actually think you're enjoying
                   this.

DOCTOR: Nonsense. But it's a puzzle, and who is better
                   suited to solving a puzzle than I? With your
                   inestimable assistance, of course.

PERI: (Grumbling)
                   Mystery? Puzzle? You make it sound like
                   Scooby Doo.

DOCTOR: Scooby Doo?

PERI: You weren't supposed to hear that.

DOCTOR: Never mind. Where are we? I think this is
            Broadway...

PERI: It is. It's the intersection of Broadway and
            Chambers Street. My mother's house is this
            way.

DOCTOR: Is it? This way.

PERI: Doctor, wait. That's the wrong way. That's
            180 degrees the wrong way from my mother's
            place.

DOCTOR: Of course it is. We're not going to your
            mother's house.

PERI: Why not?

DOCTOR: Peri, important though your mother
            undoubtedly is to you, I sincerely doubt her
            ability to cast any light upon what has
            happened here.

PERI: Maybe not, but she's still my Mom and I
            want to know she's okay.

DOCTOR: Very well. You can go home if you wish - I
            intend to head into the centre of town.

PERI: You're impossible! What's so special about
            the centre?

DOCTOR: We haven't seen anybody since we arrived. If
            there is anybody left here, they're most likely
            to congregate in a central area, don't you
            think? Emergency service, perhaps?

PERI: Maybe.

DOCTOR: And with all due respect to your mother, they are likely to know more than she about the situation.

PERI: I hate it when you're right.

DOCTOR: I'll try not to let it happen too often. You could try telephoning her. There are phone boxes over there.

PERI: We're in New York, Doctor. They're phone booths.

DOCTOR: Ridiculous! Booths, indeed! Do you have any change?

PERI: Not for this planet. You?

DOCTOR: Pounds, euros, lira, escudos...

PERI: But no American cash?

DOCTOR: Afraid not. You could always reverse the charges. Sorry, I mean, call collect.

PERI: I could - except that the phone's dead.

Phone lifted and put down.

PERI: This one, too.

DOCTOR: And this one. Looks like they're all out of order.

PERI: Maybe it's for the best. If I did get through and there was no answer, I'd only worry myself sick.

DOCTOR: Chin up. I'm sure your mother will be fine. From all you've told me she seems to be an intelligent enough woman.

PERI: So how come she married Howard?

DOCTOR: I must admit I've wondered that myself. There. That's better, isn't it? Nothing like insulting a bore to raise the spirits.

PERI: (A little cheered)
Just don't let my Mom hear you call Howard a bore. Okay, Where to?

DOCTOR: This way. I think. It's hard to tell through this snow.

PERI: When I was a kid, I always used to hope for snow so we'd get a few days off school.

DOCTOR: You would rather build a snowman than broaden your mind? Shocking.

PERI: Don't tell me you never played in the snow when you were growing up.

DOCTOR: Well, perhaps occasionally. But only occasionally, mind, though I did build the best sledge of anybody in the Academy.

PERI: I can just see you on a sledge.

DOCTOR: Shush.

PERI: Don't "shush" me.

DOCTOR: Quiet! It's difficult enough trying to hear through this wind without you babbling on.

PERI:	Thanks a lot.
DOCTOR:	It's coming from the next street along.
PERI:	I can hear it. Sort of like an elephant. Hey, slow up. Wait for me. What would elephants be doing in New York?
DOCTOR:	Careful. Stop at the corner. No need to frighten whatever they are.
PERI:	Ohmygosh. Mammoths.
DOCTOR:	It's hard to tell form this distance. They could be Mastodons. No. They've got twin, domed frontal lobes. You're quite right. Woolly Mammoths. Quite a herd, too. Thirty or forty, I'd say.
PERI:	Save the lecture, Doctor. However many there are, they're coming this way.
DOCTOR:	Good point. In that doorway. Press yourself back as flat as you can.

The herd of Mammoths lumbers by, trumpeting loudly.

PERI:	They're huge. Look at those tusks.
DOCTOR:	Designed for clearing snow so they can get to the grass underneath.
PERI:	They're gone.
DOCTOR:	Congratulations. You're the first human to see a live Mammoth since your ancestors drove them to extinction three and a half thousand years ago.

PERI: Don't blame me. I wasn't there.

A scream. A young woman, followed by the loud trumpeting bellow of a Mammoth.

PERI: Now what?

DOCTOR: It seems the city isn't so abandoned, after all. Come on.

They hurry back out into the wind. The yelling and trumpeting continue.

PERI: There. Another Mammoth.

DOCTOR: It's attacking that girl.

PERI: I don't believe it. She looks like she's wearing animal skins.

DOCTOR: What else would someone hunting Mammoths wear? Look at the way it's waving its' head around. It's clearly distressed.

PERI: It's not the only one. We have to do something before it kills her.

DOCTOR: There. Just under the shoulder.

PERI: A spear. No wonder it's wild.

Sound of another pair of feet crunching towards them. It's Alan.

ALAN: Hey! People! Thank God! I thought I was the only one left alive!

DOCTOR: Evidently you were wrong.

ALAN: I've never been so pleased to see anyone in my life. Do you have any idea what's happening here?

DOCTOR: I should have thought that was obvious.

PERI: We're on Broadway. It's been turned into a glacier and a Woolly Mammoth is attacking that girl.

ALAN: Only in New York. We've got to help her.

DOCTOR: She's safe enough in that doorway for now but she can't stay there for long. The way she's dressed, the cold will kill her if nothing else.

ALAN: We've got to move that Mammoth.

PERI: Why didn't we think of that?

ALAN: Either of you have a gun?

DOCTOR: A gun? Isn't wiping these magnificent creatures off the planet once enough for you? You want to do it again.

PERI: Take that as a "no". We're not big on guns.

DOCTOR: We have something far more useful than a mere gun.

ALAN: Sounds good to me. What is it?

DOCTOR: My vast intellect and powers of persuasion.

ALAN: What? You're going to talk nice to the Mammoth and ask it to go away and leave her alone? I don't think so.

DOCTOR: Actually, that's exactly what I'm planning to do.

ALAN: Are you nuts? Come back.

PERI: It's okay. He knows what he's doing. I hope.

The Doctor is moving towards the Mammoth - the bellowing is getting louder. The Doctor speaks calmly and in a soothing voice.

DOCTOR: It's all right. All right. Nobody's going to hurt you.

PERI: Doctor...

DOCTOR: Sssshh. Calmly now. Yes. Quietly. I'm not going to hurt you. Of course I'm not.

The Mammoth is calming.

ALAN: I don't believe it. It's working.

DOCTOR: Of course it is. I have an affinity with animals, don't I, old fellow?

Mammoth snorts a bit.

DOCTOR: Now why don't you two make yourselves useful and get that girl away from there before she turns into an icicle?

PERI: Right.

DOCTOR: And do it slowly and quietly. Any sudden movement could frighten my rather large friend here. Ssshh. There. It's all right.

PERI: Come with us. You're going to be okay now.

ALAN: I don't think she understands. Come on. It's
             okay. Come on. Take my hand. You'll be
             okay.

A grunt and a yelp of pain from the cave-girl, who will be
called Carra (explained later).

DOCTOR: Sssshhh. There. She's going. No reason for
             you for you to be upset now, is there?

PERI: No wonder she didn't want to move. Look at
             the cuts on her feet.

ALAN: Let me see.

Another yelp from Carra.

ALAN: They're not deep but there are a lot of them.
             I'd guess she's been walking on broken glass.

PERI: The Doctor should take a look at those.

ALAN: She's in luck. I am a doctor.

PERI: Actually, I meant, oh never mind.

ALAN: Yeah. These need dressed. And she needs
             clothes quick.

DOCTOR: Did I hear you say that you're a doctor?

ALAN: Yeah. Alan Rigg.

DOCTOR: I am simply known as The Doctor, and this is
             my friend, Peri. Now would you be kind
             enough to put that unfortunate girl's foot
             down and help me with this poor fellow?

ALAN: The Mammoth? I'm a doctor, not a vet.

DOCTOR: I don't care if you're a tree surgeon, just come and help me.

PERI: It's okay. I'll look after her.

ALAN: Okay, Doctor... Whatever... Dolittle. What do you want me to do?

DOCTOR: Just Doctor will do fine. We can't leave the spear in the Mammoth's shoulder. When I tell you, grab the shaft and pull the spear out.

ALAN: It'll go crazy.

DOCTOR: I assure you he won't feel a thing. Ready?

ALAN: I guess.

DOCTOR: Pull.

Alan grunts with strain and the Doctor gives a cry of pain as the spear is pulled free.

ALAN: Got it. It's a pretty clean wound.

DOCTOR: Good. It should heal quickly. Off you go. Join the rest of the herd.

A snort and the Mammoth lumbers off through the snow. The Doctor breathes heavily - he is in some pain.

PERI: Doctor?

DOCTOR: I'll be all right in a minute or two.

ALAN: What's wrong with him?

PERI: You took the pain for the Mammoth, didn't you? I don't know how, but you did.

DOCTOR: It seemed the least I could do.

PERI: Sometimes, Doctor, you remind me why I
            like you so much.

DOCTOR: Let's push on, shall we? This way.

Carra grunts and protests.

PERI: Looks like she's scared of something in that
            direction.

DOCTOR: Interesting. I wonder why. All the more
            reason to go this way. Come along.
More grunts and protests from Carra.

ALAN: Does he know what he's doing?

PERI   Most of the time.

DOCTOR   (Impatient)
            Peri!

ALAN   Aw, what the hell? Come on. It'll be okay.

Carra grunts and protests.

ALAN: I promise. Come on.

She's still not sure.

PERI: Honest. You'll be okay.

ALAN: We've got to stick together. Please. Come
            with us.

There is a roar - possible human, possibly not. Whatever, it
decides Carra's mind for her. She grunts,

ALAN: That's better. Hey, Doctor... Doctor. Why
           can't she speak?

DOCTOR: I doubt if her people have developed much
           more than a rudimentary language.

ALAN: Her people? You're saying she really is a
           cave... person?

PERI: Who else would be fighting with a
           Mammoth?

ALAN: That's nuts!

DOCTOR: As "nuts" as seeing a herd of Woolly
           Mammoths charging along a Broadway that's
           entombed in ice?

ALAN: Yeah. No. You got me there.

DOCTOR: And whatever it is in this direction that has
           this young lady so frightened, I have no doubt
           that it will be equally "nuts". And more than
           likely highly important in explaining what has
           happened here.

PERI: What's that?

DOCTOR: What? No, I hear it now.

It's the same screeching, rumbling sound from earlier - the
effect from the lab.

ALAN: No. Not again.

PERI: There. Over the square.

ALAN: It's like a whirlpool of electricity.

DOCTOR: A rift in space and time.

PERI: What?

DOCTOR: Time has been distorted and jumbled up.
            Different time periods from the same place
            are trying to simultaneously occupy the same
            position in space and time.

PERI: That's impossible. Isn't it?

DOCTOR: Not only impossible - it's disastrous as well.
            Unless we can find a way of putting this right,
            it could spread through Earth's history. It
            could mean the end of this world of yours.

Episode 2

1.
Recapping from part one.
The Doctor, Peri, Alan and Carra are on the ice-bound Broadway. The time distortion is spitting and crackling away in the distance.

DOCTOR: Time has been distorted and jumbled up.
             Different time periods from the same place
             are trying to simultaneously occupy the same
             position in space and time.

PERI: That's impossible. Isn't it?

DOCTOR: Not only impossible - it's disastrous as well.
             Unless we can find a way of putting this right,
             it could spread through Earth's history. It
             could mean the end of this world of yours.

ALAN: You're joking, right?

DOCTOR: Do I look as if I'm joking? Even a little bit?
             Believe me. This is no laughing matter.

PERI: But you know how to fix this? I mean, this is
             time, and you're a Time Lord, so this must be
             right up your alley. Right?

DOCTOR: Your faith in me is touching, Peri, but
             frankly, at the moment, I haven't got a clue.

PERI: Now I'm worried.

DOCTOR: Never fear. I'll think of something. I usually
             do. Probably something hugely clever, rather
             daring and with more than a hint of panache.

PERI:	Now I'm really worried.
DOCTOR:	What was that?
PERI:	Nothing.
DOCTOR:	Jolly good. Right. First things first, I want a look at that time distortion.

As Peri replies, there is a sort of wave sound, with a hint of the sound of the time distortion.

PERI:	Is that wi - wi -wise?
DOCTOR:	First things first, I want a look at that time distortion.
PERI:	Is that wise?

The wave sound continues.

DOCTOR:	First things first, I want a look at that time distortion.
PERI:	Is that wise?

The wave sound passes.

ALAN:	What the Hell was that?
DOCTOR:	This is worse than I thought. Time is de-stabilising. That eddy was just the beginning.
PERI:	How long do we have until things go pear-shaped?
DOCTOR:	Pear-shaped? The world is about to end - indeed possibly never have existed - and the best you can call it is pear-shaped?

PERI: Save the lecture till later - if there is a later. How   long?

DOCTOR: There's no way of telling. But I'm convinced it's more vital then ever that I see that distortion first hand. We'd better hurry.

Carra complains - she sounds terrified.

ALAN: There's no way she's going back that way. She's way too scared.

DOCTOR: I wonder what exactly she saw that has her so afraid.

ALAN: I'll ask her nicely. Maybe she'll tell me.

DOCTOR: Maybe she will at that.

PERI: I thought you said she couldn't speak.

DOCTOR: You humans haven't evolved much since her time - in some cases I'd say quite the reverse - physically she has everything she needs to talk. All she's missing is a language - and the knowledge of how to make the sounds, naturally.

ALAN: So all we have to do is teach her to speak. No sweat. That shouldn't take more than a year or three.

DOCTOR: Save your sarcasm, Doctor Kilmore. I can teach her rather more quickly than that. It's not something I would normally consider doing, but in desperate circumstances... Bring her here.

PERI: What are you going to do?

DOCTOR: Augment her mind a little.

ALAN: Augment her mind? What is he talking about?

PERI: Like you took away the Mammoth's pain,
            you're going to plant language in her head.

DOCTOR: More or less.

PERI: You do remember what happened last time
            we met somebody who'd been augmented?

DOCTOR: This will be different - hopefully. I'm not
            changing anything in her personality, just
            giving her a voice.

ALAN: That's imposs... ah, hell. After all I've seen
            today, what's one more impossibility?

DOCTOR: That's probably the most sensible thing
            you've said since we met.

ALAN: (Quietly, to Carra)
            It's okay. This won't hurt. Will it?

DOCTOR: I shouldn't think so.

ALAN: Shouldn't think so? You don't know?

DOCTOR: It's hardly the sort of thing I do every day.
            Now do be quiet. This takes a great deal of
            concentration.
            (Gently, to Carra)
            Now then, it's all right.

She grunts nervously.

DOCTOR: This won't hurt. You'll be all right. Keep still.
            This won't work if we break contact.

Carra grunts and whimpers in a little distress.

ALAN:	You said this wouldn't hurt.
PERI:	Quiet. He knows what he's doing.
DOCTOR:	(Breathing a little heavily) There. It's done. How do you feel?

No answer.

DOCTOR:	Do you understand? How do you feel?

When Carra speaks, she is faltering and unsure. Her accent is English - like the Doctor's.

CARRA:	Cold... feet... not feel feet.
DOCTOR:	Numb with the cold, poor thing. Here, take my cloak.
ALAN:	Woh!
DOCTOR:	Yes?
ALAN:	Nice coat.
DOCTOR:	High fashion should not be ridiculed by a man wearing brown corduroy trousers and tan cowboy boots. Now then young lady. What did you see that has you so frightened, hmm?
CARRA:	Light.
PERI:	What kind of light?
DOCTOR:	That one? The one in the sky?
CARRA:	Not that. Like same as that but small.

DOCTOR: A smaller disruption?

CARRA: Blue spin light. People get old. Get young. People go away...

ALAN: Go away?

PERI: They disappear?

CARRA: Disappear. Yes. Disappear and go away.

PERI: Where do you think they go?

DOCTOR: A more likely question would be "when do they go to?" First order must be to see this distortion. Can you show me where it is?

CARRA: Which? Many blue lights near.

DOCTOR: Are there indeed? The closest one.

CARRA: Not safe. We will hurt us.

DOCTOR: We'll hurt worse if we don't sort this out. You must show me.

ALAN: Leave her alone. Can't you see how scared she is?

CARRA: Show you. Here way.

DOCTOR: Thank you.

PERI: (Quietly)
Doctor, she's trying to hide it but she really is terrified.

DOCTOR: I don't blame her. I'm a bit nervous myself.

PERI: Thanks. That makes me feel a lot better!

CARRA: Light here.

ALAN: It must be round the corner of this building...

As they turn the corner, there's the sound of a small version of the distortion effect.

DOCTOR: Stay back.

ALAN: My God.

PERI: It's beautiful.

DOCTOR: Let's have a closer look. No, you all stay
                back.

PERI: What is it?

A crackle from the distortion.

DOCTOR: Apart from unstable? Touchy, isn't it?
                Actually, it's not all that significant in itself,
                it's just a focus point.

PERI: For what?

DOCTOR: Time. It's a point in space with enough
                chronometric gravity to pull temporal
                particles together.

ALAN: Do you understand any of this?

PERI: Not really, but then when do I ever? In
                English, Doctor.

DOCTOR: In all the confusion in time, this is a stable
                nexus point where times intersect, rather than

are just smashed together. In fact, if I get closer, I may just get a peek through into another time zone.

PERI: Be careful.

DOCTOR: When am I ever anything else? There. I think I can see, yes, definitely a man. He's unconscious. Or dead. No, he's breathing.

PERI: Doctor, that thing's getting antsy.

DOCTOR: Just a little closer. Hello? HELLO? Can you hear me?

PERI: Get away from that there.

The distortion sounds louder and angrier.

DOCTOR: I think you might be right. Maybe I...
The distortion sounds louder again.

PERI: Doctor!

DOCTOR: Get back! Go back!

ALAN: Come on!

The distortion sounds louder still.

PERI: DOCTOR!

The sound fades away.

PERI: DOCTOR!

ALAN: He's gone.

PERI: I can see that! I'm not blind! DOCTOR!

The sound disappears completely.

CARRA: Light is gone.

ALAN: The Doctor said it was unstable.

PERI: It's completely gone. How can we get him back?

ALAN: Hell, we don't even know where he is.

PERI: There must be something I can do. What would the Doctor do?

She thinks for a moment then sighs.

PERI: We'd get her in out of the blizzard before she freezes to death.

CARRA: Cold.

PERI: Doctor, where are you?

2.
Jungle.
The Doctor arrives, yelling and shouting in the distortion sound.

DOCTOR: Go back!

He lands with an audible and painful thump in the foliage.

DOCTOR: What an unpleasant mode of transport! Peri?

Sound of the distortion fades, replaced with jungle noises.

DOCTOR: No, wait. Never mind. What are things coming to when I start talking to a tempero-spacial anomaly?

A groan from the man he saw earlier - it's Broxton.

DOCTOR: Oh. I'd almost forgotten about you? Come on,
               wake up. Wake up, man.

BROXTON: What... abandon the base! Secure the lab!

DOCTOR: Do calm down, there's a good chap.
               Whatever your problem was, you've got
               bigger ones now... oh, General.

BROXTON: John Broxton, US Army. Where the Hell am
               I?

DOCTOR: At a wild guess, I'd say we're in New York.

BROXTON: You're crazy. Look at the forest. It's tropical.
               There's nothing like this in New York.

DOCTOR: Not in 1985 - you are from 1985, I take it?

BROXTON: What kind of a dumb-ass question is that? Of
               course I'm from 1985.

DOCTOR: For your information, I am not given to
               asking "dumb-ass" questions, as you so
               colourfully put it. And as for our location -
               it's definitely more a question of when than
               of where.

BROXTON: When? I don't follow.

DOCTOR: Of course you don't. You're a soldier.
               Temporal entropy theory is hardly your
               department, but I'll explain as quickly as I
               can - and to save a few moments can we just
               take your protestations of incredulity as
               given?

BROXTON: Military Intelligence is not necessarily an oxymoron, Mr...

DOCTOR: Just "Doctor" will do. Very well, in plain terms, the fabric of space/time has been disturbed and has begun a domino effect which may destroy everything on the Earth, past, present and future.

BROXTON: Everything?

DOCTOR: It may very well be as though the Earth never existed.

BROXTON: How do you know all this?

DOCTOR: That would take rather a long time to explain and I doubt if you would believe me even if I was in the mood to tell you.

BROXTON: Well, Doctor, I suggest you get in the mood to tell me, pretty damn quick.

DOCTOR: Must you really punctuate every sentence with an oath?

There is a roar - a big, scary roar.

BROXTON: What was that?

DOCTOR: Taking into account the temperature and nature of the fauna, I'd say we're in the late Cretatious Period and that is most likely Tyrannosaurus Rex, roughly fifty yards that way and heading straight for us.

BROXTON: Congratulations. You are undoubtedly the biggest loon I've met in my entire life. No wonder you wear a clown's coat.

Another roar and the crashing of trees.

DOCTOR: Quickly. Out of sight. Keep down.

The T Rex lumbers by.

BROXTON: Oh, my God.

DOCTOR: You were saying?

BROXTON: It really is a T Rex.

DOCTOR: Well, it's not a French Poodle. Once it's
                 moved on a little, I would suggest another
                 colourful oath.

BROXTON: Run like hell?

DOCTOR: That's the one.

3.
New York.
The blizzard is still blowing and is becoming almost
unbearable.

ALAN: The blizzard's getting worse. Peri, we have to
                 get her inside. She's almost unconscious.

Carra grunts. There is a roar, the same as Carra heard in part 1.
Now we hear it properly, it's clear that it's human. Human,
wild and very annoyed.

ALAN: What's that?

PERI: Back there. It's one of her people.

Carra is not pleased by this turn of events. Whoever this man
is, he's not her favourite person.

CARRA: Run fast now.

Another roar.

ALAN: Whoever he is, she doesn't like him much.

The roars are getting closer.

PERI: He's spotted us - and he doesn't look too
            happy either.

ALAN: She's terrified of him. What does he want?

CARRA: Me. For mate.

PERI: And you don't want him?

Huge roar.

PERI: Can't say I blame you.

CARRA: Run fast.

More bellows.

PERI: We can't let him take her.

ALAN: Any ideas on how we stop him? He's huge.

PERI: Don't tell me - you're a wimp?

ALAN: A doormat.

PERI: Run.

ALAN: Too late.

The Caveman roars aggressively.

PERI   Duck.

Caveman smacks down on the bonnet of a car.

ALAN: That was close.

PERI: Didn't do the car's hood any favours either.
                Listen. She's not interested.

Another roar.

ALAN: Don't get too close - he might decide on you
                instead of her.

PERI: In his dreams.

Another roar. The caveman is furious.

ALAN: Can't we talk about this?

Another roar and the sound of Alan being grabbed.

ALAN: I guess not.

Sound of a scuffle. Alan is being choked.

PERI: Let him go.

She yelps as she's thrown away by the roaring caveman.

CARRA: No. Not for you.

It's her turn to be swatted away.

PERI: No wonder you don't get any girls.

ALAN: (Being choked)
                Get him off. He's choking me.

PERI: Find something to hit him with.

CARRA: This.

PERI: Too light.

The caveman's roaring continues.

ALAN: (Choking)
               Hurry.

PERI: The car's bumper is loose. Help me get it
               free.

The sound of Alan being choked is joined by the bending of
metal.

PERI: Nearly. Another pull. Got it.

The caveman roars in pain as he is whacked with the bumper.
Alan is dropped to the ground.

ALAN: (Struggling for breath)
               His knee. Hit his knee.

Another whack. The roars get worse, and with another whack
the caveman topples into the snow, howling with pain. Carra
joins in the hitting. She sounds like she's enjoying it. The
caveman roars some more. The sound of a car door opening
and then the door slams off the caveman's skull a couple of
time and he hits the ground out cold.

ALAN: He's out cold. Where did you learn that trick
               with the car door?

PERI: High School dating. If we leave him out here
               he'll freeze. Help me put him in the car.

Grunts as they heave the caveman.

ALAN: There. Nearly.

A head thumps on the side of the door.

PERI: Sorry. Actually, no I'm not. He's in.

ALAN: He hasn't missed many dinners.

PERI: Shut the door.

ALAN: I can't with her in the way.

Sound of Carra giving the caveman a final whack. Then the
door slams shut.

ALAN: That's what you get for messing with a New
               York girl. Where to now?

PERI: The Mall. There. It doesn't look like it's been
               too badly affected by the ice. Go in there.

ALAN: By the time sleeping beauty wakes up the
               snow will have covered our tracks.

Sound of them crunching through the snow in the blizzard.

PERI: Watch the glass. Her feet are bad enough
               already.

ALAN: I'll carry her.

He grunts as he picks Carra up. Broken glass crunches under
their feet as they walk over it.

PERI: This is weird. It's kinda creepy. The last time
               I was in here, I could hardly move for people.

No answer.

PERI: I said. Never mind. You could put her down now, you know. We're passed the broken glass.

ALAN: What? No, it's okay. Poor kid's almost wiped out anyway.

PERI: Suit yourself. It's just as well these stores are open. We're gonna need food.

ALAN: And heat. If we don't find a way of warming her up she'll be in big trouble.

PERI: There's a camping store over there. We can find stoves and heaters in there.

ALAN: A couple of sleeping bags would be handy as well.

PERI: Yeah. Wait a minute. I've had a better idea. We'll get what we need from the camping store, pick up some food, then head to Milford and Greenes.

ALAN: Milford and... the furniture place?

PERI: If I'm gonna sit out that blizzard, I'm at least going to do it on something comfortable. Besides, I think I might know a way of stopping your new girlfriend catching hypothermia.

ALAN: Hey. She's not my girlfriend, okay? On the other hand, this is the longest relationship I've had in three years, so what the hell?

PERI: Come on.

4.
The Jungle.
The Doctor and Broxton are making their way through the foliage.

BROXTON: Is there a purpose to our wandering through
            the jungle like this, Doctor, or are you just
            giving me the ten cent tour of pre-history?

DOCTOR: General, of course there's a reason for us
            moving this way - I just haven't worked out
            what it is yet.

BROXTON: I hope at least one of us understood that,
            because it meant nothing to me.

DOCTOR: When I was back in 1985, I was told that
            there were a number of those small distortions
            across the city. Now if one of them could
            send me here...

BROXTON: Another one might send us back to 1985?

DOCTOR: Or to almost any other time you care to
            mention.

BROXTON: You mean you can't be sure?

DOCTOR: (Cheerfully)
            No.

BROXTON: So we could wind up at the end of time - or
            back when the world was still a ball of molten
            rock.

DOCTOR: Or earlier - before the Earth was here at all.
            Perhaps back to before the universe was born.

BROXTON: Maybe using one of those disturbance things isn't such a good idea.

DOCTOR: Of course it is. Can you think of a better way back to your time? No, didn't think so. I've found that even in chaos, the universe has a way of establishing some kind of order. The fact that the link between times was strong enough for me to get through unscathed makes me think that there are only a few time periods currently connected.

BROXTON: But there will be more.

DOCTOR: Oh, undoubtedly. Which is a second good reason for us to find a one of these time rifts.

BROXTON: Second? I thought that would be top of the list.

DOCTOR: I can't be sure but I think I saw a couple of little dinosaurs following us who would be number one.

BROXTON: What? I don't see them.

DOCTOR: Maybe my eyes were playing tricks on me.

A rustle in the undergrowth.

DOCTOR: On the other hand, I have perfect eyesight which has never failed me yet. Shall we go?

BROXTON: I'm right in front of you.

They hurry off, pushing through the undergrowth. Their noise fades away. After a few seconds, the undergrowth moves again, and there is the chittering sound of a number of small dinosaurs.

5.
The New York Mall.
Alan has been left on cooking duty. He's scraping the contents
of a little pot onto plates.

ALAN: You finished in there?

PERI: (Calling)
               Nearly. Hey. Cut that out! I'm soaked enough
               already.

ALAN: If you kiddies have finished splashing in the
               pool, food's ready. Not edible, but ready and
               hot.

PERI: Give us a second. Dry yourself off.

ALAN: I could help, you know.

PERI: You stay on that side of the screen, bucko.
               She's capable of drying herself.

ALAN: Hey, I'm a doctor.

PERI: You're not *her* doctor. There. Done. Here,
               now. Get the cloak back around you.

Bare feet slap on the floor.

ALAN: Hi. Here's your food. Don't expect much.
               There's only so much you can do with a
               couple of camping stoves. Especially after
               they've worked overtime filling a bath with
               hot water.

PERI: You agreed that a warm bath was the best
               way to heat her up again.

Carra sniffs at the food.

PERI: It's okay. You can eat it.

ALAN: Just don't expect to enjoy it.

With loud and uncouth sound effects, Carra starts eating - with
her hands.

ALAN: Whoa. Slow down.

PERI: You'll choke yourself. Take it slowly. Try
                   using the spoon. That thing on the plate.

CARRA: Spoon? This?

PERI: That's it.

Sound of spoon scraping on the plate - an unpleasant
screeching sound.

PERI: Well, everything takes practice, I suppose.
                   Did you get what you need from the drug
                   store?

ALAN: Everything. It felt kinda weird just taking
                   stuff without paying for it.

PERI: In the circumstances, I'm sure a judge would
                   let you off easy.

ALAN: Let's see your feet.

Carra grunts again.

CARRA: Feet hurt. Feel now.

ALAN: I'm going to fix them, okay?

CARRA: Okay.

PERI: How bad are they?

ALAN: The cuts aren't too deep. They'll heal in a few
                   days. It's a miracle she hasn't got frostbite.

PERI: We'll have to find clothes for her. She can't
                   go back out there in just that cloak and her
                   own whatever you call that skin thing she was
                   wearing, is soaked - she got a bit excited at
                   her first bath.

ALAN: So I heard. This ointment is gonna sting
                   some.

Carra yelps in pain.

ALAN: It'll only hurt for a minute. After that, it'll
                   make the pain go away.

CARRA: (Grunt that pretty much says "I hope so".)

ALAN: This dressing will stop the cuts from getting
                   infected.

PERI: You're good at this. Which hospital do you
                   work at?

ALAN: Saint Pete's. I work ER mainly. I'm just glad
                   to be doing something normal here. This is all
                   so screwed.

PERI: It is pretty bad.

ALAN: Pretty bad? How can you be so calm? You
                   sound like this happens every day.

PERI: Actually, you'd be surprised. With the
                   Doctor, nothing's ever dull.

ALAN: Do you think he's okay?

PERI: I hope so. He usually finds a way out of his
                problems. He's not as gruff as he likes to
                make out, you know. It's all bluster - most of
                the time. He's really a nice, sweet guy
                underneath.

6.
The jungle.
The Doctor is bellowing at Broxton.

DOCTOR: IMBECILE! You could have killed us both.

BROXTON: How was I supposed to know the jungle
                ended in a sheer drop?

DOCTOR: If I might suggest in future, you could try
                opening your eyes! I could have broken
                something vital, not to mention painful.

BROXTON: How about aiming your eyes at the top of the
                rise we fell down?

DOCTOR: Ah. Oh dear. Our little dinosaur shadows...

BROXTON: Have brought some of their friends.

DOCTOR: They must be pack hunters. Too small to do
                any damage singly, but a group of them? The
                flesh would be off our bones before you could
                snap your fingers, always assuming they
                hadn't bitten your fingers off.

BROXTON: At least they seem stuck at the top of the rise.
                It's too high for them to jump.

DOCTOR:	I wouldn't count on that holding them up for long. This is their home-pitch, remember. If there's a way down, they'll find it.
BROXTON:	Are you always this cheerful?
DOCTOR:	Come on. If we put enough distance between us and them, they may lose the trail.

7.
New York Mall.
Peri, Alan and Carra have moved on and are now getting clothes for Carra.

| ALAN: | I'll go get winter jackets while you get the rest of her clothes. |

Carra moans disapproval at Alan leaving.

PERI:	He's not going far. He'll be back in a few minutes. Great. Just my luck. A cave-woman with a crush.
CARRA:	Crush? Crush like squeeze?
PERI:	Whether he winds up as your squeeze or not is your business. All I'm interested in right now is getting you dressed. Yep. That's right. Now the trousers. Your feet go in the holes. No, the one at the top. Yeah. The big one. No, just one leg in each of the trouser legs. Wait! Wait! Turn them round. The zip's at the front.
CARRA:	Zip? What is zip?
PERI:	The metal runner thing. Just grab the tab and pull it up.

Zip closing.

PERI: We've really got to work on your English. Typical of the Doctor - disappearing and leaving me to finish off the tough stuff. Here. Put this shirt on.

Snapping sound.

PERI: Get rid of the tags before they itch you to death. Hey, not bad. We'd better get you a sweater and some hiking boots. Your feet aren't much bigger than mine - say a size three.

CARRA: Trousers on legs? Shirt on body? Yes?

PERI: Yep. This sweater should do. This goes over your shirt.

CARRA: This is what?

PERI: Oh. That? That's... something your mother should have explained. It's almost the end of the world and I'm not up to explaining bras. Just bag it. I'll explain it later. Much, much later. Here. Try these socks and boots.

CARRA: Socks and boots go on feet.

PERI: That's right.

CARRA: No. Socks and boots go on <u>my</u> feet.

ALAN: How's the shopping going?

PERI: Pretty well. I hope your credit card's in good shape.

ALAN: Left it at home. Sorry.

PERI:	Too bad. Write an IOU. Sign it Donald Trump.
ALAN:	Why not? I never liked him anyway.
CARRA:	I have a bra.
ALAN:	You don't say.
PERI:	Actually, she's saying a lot. She's discovered personal pronouns, and now she's putting together sentences. Whatever the Doctor did to her head, it's really starting to kick in.
CARRA:	(Worried) Cat.
PERI:	No need to be insulting.
CARRA:	Near us. A cat is near. Not knife cat. Knife tooth. What is the word? Sabre?
PERI:	A sabre-toothed cat? Where?
CARRA:	Near. I hear the cat.
ALAN:	Oh, hell. I see the cat.
PERI:	So do I. Oh, no. There's two of them. They're huge. Run. Come on. Move it.

They run. Sound of cats following them, snarling. These are hungry cats.

ALAN:	They're catching us.
PERI:	Head back to the escalator.

Another snarl of a sabre-tooth.

ALAN:	Damn. One them's cut us off.

PERI:	The staircase! That way!

More snarls. Alan grunts as he turfs anything he can get hold of back in the path of the cats.

PERI:	Forget throwing things at them. Just keep running.

CARRA:	Stop.

ALAN:	Keep going. Go down the stairs.

PERI:	Aw, hell.

CARRA:	Stairs are ice.

ALAN:	The front of this side of the mall's shattered. The stairs are sheer ice.

PERI:	It'd be like trying to run on glass.

The cats roar again, closer this time.

PERI:	They've cut us off. We're trapped.

The cats roar again.

Episode 3

1.
New York Mall.
Recapping from the end of part 2.
Peri, Alan and Carra are on the run from the sabre-toothed cats.

ALAN:	Keep going. Go down the stairs.
PERI:	Aw, hell.
CARRA:	Stairs are ice.
ALAN:	The front of this side of the mall's shattered. The stairs are sheer ice.
PERI:	It'd be like trying to run on glass.

The cats roar again, closer this time.

PERI:	They've cut us off. We're trapped.

The cats roar again.

ALAN:	Is it just me or do they sound really hungry?
PERI:	You'd be hungry if you hadn't eaten in ten thousand years.
ALAN:	Yeah, but I wouldn't be trying to eat me. Get back.

He grunts as he throws anything he can find at the cats, who snarl and spit.

PERI:	I didn't some all this way home just to wind up as a cat's dinner.

ALAN:	Well, if you've got any smart ideas, I'd like to hear them real soon. I'm running out of Christmas knick-knacks to throw at these things.
PERI:	I'm thinking. I'm... you any good at sledging?
ALAN:	Nice idea but we don't have a sledge.
PERI:	True - but that door that's been knocked off its' hinges should be big enough for three.
ALAN:	You're crazy. It'll never work.
PERI:	Suit yourself. Personally, I'd rather break my neck than be eaten alive by those cats.
ALAN:	Good point.
PERI:	Keep them busy while we get the door.
ALAN:	Anything else? World peace and global harmony?
CARRA:	Throw things!
PERI:	Couldn't have said it better myself. Help me with the door.

Peri and Carra grunt as they move the heavy door.

CARRA:	The door is heavy.
PERI:	We'll manage.
ALAN:	Hurry it up. This is the last present I have for these tabbies.

The door thumps down.

PERI: There. Done.

CARRA: Come now.

ALAN: Coming.

PERI: Get on.

ALAN: Done.

PERI: Everybody holding tight? Too bad if you're not. Push.

Sounds of grunting and shoving as the door starts.

ALAN: They're getting closer.

PERI: Hold on. Here goes.

The cats are snarling and closer. They door scrapes and scrunches over the edge of the stairs and begins to slide down, sounding like a bob-sleigh on a down-hill run. The door's passengers whoop and yell and the door skids down the stairs.

ALAN: We're going too fast. We'll never make the corner.

PERI: Use your feet. We'll make it if we all push against the railing. Push. Now. Push.

Their feet thump against the railings as the door skids down the ice.

ALAN: It's working.

PERI: Nearly.

ALAN: We've done it.

PERI: Keep holding on. It's downhill from here.

They gives more whoops and cheers as the door slides on down the ice, picking up speed.

CARRA: We move faster.

PERI: No more turns to slow us down.

ALAN: Just one thing - does this door have brakes?

PERI: Don't ask me. I'm a botanist, not a tobogganist.

The sound changes a little, signifying the change from iced stairs to icy floor.

ALAN: We're down - but we're not slowing.

PERI: Lean to the right. Not too much. If we miss the open door we'll crash straight through the glass front.

The door skids on.

PERI: A little more. More.

Again, the sound changes. The howling of the wind joins the sound of the door on the ice.

ALAN: We made it.

CARRA: Not stopping.

PERI: Hold tight. We're gonna hit that snowdrift.

Howls and yells as the door whumps into a snowdrift.

PERI: Everybody okay?

ALAN:	That was great. Let's do it again.

PERI:	Maybe later. How about you?

When Carra speaks, it's clear that though speaking is new to her, she is rapidly progressing. It should be a bit unnerving, but also rather sweet. (If that mixture makes any sense.)

CARRA:	No pain. Cats will follow. (Thoughtful, correcting herself carefully) The cats will follow. We should go far from here.
PERI:	Sounds like a plan to me.

ALAN:	I don't believe it.

PERI:	Now what?

ALAN:	Thank God. There. It's a truck.

PERI:	Heading this way. Hey.

The truck is closer and can now be heard.

ALAN:	Hey. Stop. Slow down, there.

PERI:	They're not stopping.

ALAN:	They've got to. HEY! STOP! HEY!

PERI:	Got off the road. They're not stopping.

ALAN:	Dammit, STOP!

PERI:	Alan, move!

The truck is now very close - almost on top of him. Very loud.

CARRA:	Move!

Sound of Alan being knocked out of harm's way into the snow by Carra.

ALAN: S.O.B.'s. They would have run me down.

PERI: They would have, too, if she hadn't tackled you. You could have a career with the Jets.

ALAN: Thanks. You probably saved my life.

CARRA: I do not want you died. Dead.

ALAN: I don't want me died either.

Sound of them getting back to their feet.

ALAN: Why the hell didn't they stop?

PERI: I guess there's only one way to find out. Follow them.

2.
70 Million years ago.
The Doctor and Broxton are still walking.

BROXTON: any sign of... whatever it is you're looking for, Doctor?

DOCTOR: Not yet, General, but I'm sure it can't be far away.

BROXTON: I hope not. Not that I miss the jungle or anything, but I don't like being on an open plain like this.

DOCTOR: No cover?

BROXTON: Exactly.

DOCTOR: Look on the bright side. At least a huge,
            ravenous carnivore can't creep up on us and
            catch us unawares out here.

BROXTON: Talking of carnivores...

DOCTOR: Yes, I spotted our little friends were back
            behind us. But at least the open plain has
            them keeping their distance.
            (Thoughtfully)
            Have you noticed anything odd about this
            grass?

BROXTON: Not really - but from the tone of your voice I
            take it you have.

DOCTOR: Unless I'm very much mistaken - which I
            might add I very rarely am - this grass comes
            from a time period around forty or forty-five
            million years after the dinosaurs were wiped
            out.

BROXTON: Maybe you're just mistaken.

DOCTOR: Don't be absurd...

A quick swooshing of the time distortion effect.

DOCTOR: ... this grass comes from a time period around
            forty or forty-five million years after the
            dinosaurs were wiped out.

BROXTON: Maybe you're just mistaken.

DOCTOR: Don't be absurd. Wait a minute.

BROXTON: Didn't we just...

DOCTOR: Repeat ourselves? Actually, this could explain why the jungle ended so abruptly.

BROXTON: I have no idea what you're talking about, but feel free to enlighten me at any time.

DOCTOR: Isn't it obvious? Evidently not. The ripples in time we've been experiencing have a side effect of the affected time zones squashed together.

BROXTON: Which I guess is a bad sign.

DOCTOR: You could say that. It means more and more time zones are trying to co-exist at one point in time and space.

BROXTON: Then what?

DOCTOR: Most likely, then nothing. Think of time as being like a huge, multi-dimesional elastic band. What happens if you stretch and twist and pull at an elastic band?

BROXTON: It stretches, obviously.

DOCTOR: And then what?

BROXTON: It snaps.

DOCTOR: Exactly. Just as an elastic band would snap back into place, time will try to snap back to its' regular flow.

BROXTON: Something tells me that isn't as good news as it sounds.

DOCTOR: Indeed not. When an elastic band snaps back, the most you get is stung fingers. The energy released by time getting back on track could be enough to tear the Earth apart. It would certainly blow a hole the size of continental America in the planet.

BROXTON: How many fatalities will there be?

DOCTOR: The energy release will be at the originating point of the disturbance, both in space and time.

BROXTON: New York, 1985.

DOCTOR: Yes. I think it would be quicker to count the survivors than the casualties. Unfortunately, I don't think it would take long.

BROXTON: What could have caused this?

DOCTOR: Any number of this, I suppose. A bit of super-string colliding with the Earth, a mini black hole. It could even have been a transient wormhole opening one end of its' conduit on the planet.

BROXTON: What about an experiment on Earth? Say, someone trying to warp space to transport matter.

DOCTOR: Oh, yes. That could have done it, though anyone trying to do that without taking into consideration the effects space warping has on time would have to be a complete and utter idiot.

A moment of realisation.

DOCTOR: You're a complete and utter idiot aren't you?

BROXTON: So it would appear.

DOCTOR: What on Earth were you thinking about?

BROXTON: Doing my job.

DOCTOR: I thought your job was to protect your country not wipe it off the face of the planet.

BROXTON: I'm more than aware of my failings, Doctor. Now suppose you tell me how you know so much about how time works?

DOCTOR: Let's just say that I'm a professional. Time is my business.

BROXTON: That's not good enough.

DOCTOR: I'm afraid it'll have to be. Take a look at our little dinosaur friends.

The dinosaurs are chittering nervously.

BROXTON: Something's got them spooked.

DOCTOR: I really don't want to stay around to find out what that is, do you?

BROXTON: Good point.

Sound of them hurrying through the grass, and then there is a gentle sort of swoosh in the air, just for a second.

BROXTON: What in the hell was that?

DOCTOR: It felt like the air was disturbed by something passing right beside us.

BROXTON: A side-effect of the time distortion?

DOCTOR: Must have been. Odd, though. Still, we can worry about that later. Keep going.

BROXTON: I'd still like to know what it was.

3.
A small, echoing room.
When the first voice speaks it is clearly mechanical. The second sounds almost human, though thinner and reedier. This is the Scout (he'll be explained in a little while.)

ROBOT: Target identified and located.

SCOUt: Good. Do nothing. Keep the target under observation but do not harm him.

ROBOT: Instructions received and understood.

SCOUT: We do not harm others - but we must survive ourselves.

4.
New York.
It still a blizzard.
Peri, Alan and Carra have tracked down the truck that almost killed them.

ALAN: One good thing about all this snow - it makes following the truck easy.

CARRA: Snow makes tracking hard to hide. Every member of my tribe learns this early. We will find this ... lorry...? truck soon.

PERI: There it is. In front of the those stores. No wonder they wouldn't stop for us.

ALAN: Looters. I don't believe it - Armageddon's about to hit and all they can think of ripping off TVs.

PERI: Who are they gonna sell them to? The Mammoths? Leave them to it. They won't be able to help us.

ALAN: But I guess they can hurt us. They've seen us.

Gunshots sound, ricocheting off ice and exposed stonework.

PERI: Get down.

Sound of them all hitting the snow. More gunshots.

ALAN: Behind that car.

Sound of them scrambling behind the car and more gunshots.

PERI: It won't take them long to get here.

ALAN: Maybe they'll lose interest.

More gunshots.

ALAN: Maybe not.

PERI: If anybody's got any ideas, I'm all ears.

CARRA: Something is coming. Not men with guns. Not a truck either.

The roar of an engine - a powerful one and a large vehicle moving through the snow.

ALAN: Police!

PERI: That's a SWAT team's armoured car.

ON THE SHELF

A policeman (Barker) speaks over the vehicle's PA.

BARKER: Throw down your weapons and surrender immediately. Resistance will be met with deadly force.

The looters open fire on the SWAT vehicle. More ricochets.

PERI: Stay down! There's more chance of a ricochet getting us than any of the looters.

The SWAT vehicle closes and they return fire. A door is heard opening.

BARKER: Go, go, go.

A loud and close ricochet whizzes by Alan.

ALAN: Jesus!

BARKER: Hey, Collins. Back it up a ways.

Vehicle backs up.

BARKER: I thought I saw you hiding there. From they way they were taking pot-shots at you I assume you're not part of their gang.

PERI: Absolutely not.

ALAN: They tried to run us down a few blocks back. We followed them here.

BARKER: My guys have it pretty much under control now. You'd better get in here. You'll be safer back at the camp. You might not be so lucky next time.

PERI: Next time? There are more looters out there?

BARKER: There's nothing like misery to bring out the worst in people. Come on up.

CARRA: Looters? People who take from shops without paying?
(Thoughtfully)
Then we are...

PERI: (Interrupting)
Glad you came by. It's dangerous enough out there without looters shooting at us.

BARKER: Give me a minute to check with my guys then we'll move out.

Sound of Barker dropping to the snow outside.

PERI: (Quietly)
Just as well we cut those tags off, huh?

CARRA: Why...

PERI: Shush. Alan will explain later.

ALAN: I will?

BARKER: (Clambering back in)
We've rounded up the lot of them. Let's get moving before we freeze here.

5.
On the plain, millions of years ago.
The Doctor and Broxton are hurrying along. The Doctor is rather puffing by now.

BROXTON: Feeling the pace, Doctor? This is quite a hill.

DOCTOR: I'll manage, thank you, General. I'm just not as young as I once was.

BROXTON: Who is?

DOCTOR: I have been - on several occasions.

BROXTON: Not for the first time, I have no idea what you're talking about.

DOCTOR: (Triumphant)
Ha! There.

Sound of the time distortion. It's big this time.

BROXTON: Dear Lord.

DOCTOR: I suppose it is impressive if you like that sort of thing. Shall we?

BROXTON: Shall we what? We're not going near that thing?

DOCTOR: It's the only way. You do want to get back to 1985?

BROXTON: Yes, but...

DOCTOR: General, you have precisely two choices. One, you come with me through the time disturbance back to 1985, where we try to find a way of putting time back on her proper path, or two, you stay here and most probably wind up as lunch for those little carnivorous dinosaurs who've been tracking us.

BROXTON: When you put it like that, I don't really have a choice, do I?

DOCTOR: I thought you'd see it like that. Talking of those dinosaurs, they seem to be getting even more nervous.

BROXTON: They're not alone. Let's get this over with.

6.
The scout's room.
He is getting another report from his robot.

ROBOT: Target has discovered time rift.

SCOUT: Take no action.

ROBOT: Warning. Target will use time rift to return to
           1985.

SCOUT: Let him. Even is he returns to his own period,
           there is nothing he can do. If he is to die, at
           least he can die in his own time. Maintain
           surveillance then return to ship for time-jump.

ROBOT: Instructions received and understood.

7.
The plain.
The Doctor and Broxton are rushing towards the distortion.
There is another mild swoosh as the air is disturbed.

BROXTON: There it is again.

DOCTOR: Odd. It was heading towards the disturbance.
            I'll think about it later.

The sound of the disturbance is now quite pronounced.

BROXTON: What do we do? Walk into thing thing?

DOCTOR: Exactly.

BROXTON: Okay. Here goes.

DOCTOR: Not so fast! Hasn't your impatience got you into enough trouble for one day? Look into the distortion.

BROXTON: I can see... what? Images of what?

DOCTOR: The different time periods that are linked together. If we jump in at the wrong time we'll miss 1985 and wind up who knows when.

BROXTON: I hope this thing tunes itself into 1985 quick, Doctor. We've got company.

DOCTOR: Company?

The dinosaurs are chittering very nervously.

DOCTOR: Odd. I'd have thought they would have been too frightened by the distortion to come this close.

A giant roar - a T Rex.

BROXTON: That T Rex explain everything?

DOCTOR: Absolutely. I've got it worked out. It's running a cycle through the time zones.

The roars are getting louder.

BROXTON: They're getting closer, Doctor.

DOCTOR: I can see that. A few seconds more .A few seconds... come on.

BROXTON: Straight in?

DOCTOR: In! Now!

BROXTON: I hope you know what you're doing. Here
             goes.

With a yell he leaps into the distortion after the Doctor.

8.
1684.
A Dutch settler (Jacob) is observing the distortion in his zone.

JACOB: What is this? Never have I seen the like. Not
             even in the pages of the Holy Bible. It is the
             work of Lucifer, I say.

With a thump the Doctor arrives, followed a second later by a
yelling Broxton.

DOCTOR: That really is an uncomfortable way to travel.

BROXTON: We're alive.

DOCTOR: Must you state the obvious? Hang on, this
             isn't 1985.

BROXTON: You don't say. What was that about stating
             the obvious?

JACOB: Demons!

DOCTOR: Hello. Sorry to drop in like this.

JACOB: Are you demons or devils?

DOCTOR: Actually, I'm the Doctor and my...
             acquaintance is a soldier.

JACOB: A soldier of Satan, I say.

DOCTOR: And I say would you mind putting that
               pitchfork down before you do someone a
               mischief with it?

JACOB: You'll come with me to the town, demon.

DOCTOR: For the last time, I am not a demon - and I
               don't have time for this. Ready to go again,
               General?

BROXTON: You bet.

DOCTOR: Nearly. Now.

JACOB: Stop, demons! They're gone.

Sounds of disappearing feet, scampering off into the distance.
Jacob is legging it.

JACOB: Demons!

9.
New York. 1985
From inside the time distortion, the Doctor and Broxton are
ejected back into the blizzard. This time they land less heavily
in the snow, though there are still a few oofs and grunts as the
two land.

DOCTOR: Get off.

BROXTON: Sorry. Thanks for breaking the fall.

DOCTOR: You'll pardon me if I don't say it was a
               pleasure.

BROXTON: Bad news. We're in the wrong time again.

DOCTOR: I'm afraid not. This is how 1985 was when I
               left it. Time zones crunching together.

BROXTON: My God. Where is everybody?

DOCTOR: Scattered through time, most likely. Or in
             between time periods until time sorts itself
             out.

BROXTON: But they are alive.

DOCTOR: Probably, but there's no real way of knowing.

BROXTON: My wife was in the city when this happened.
             What have I done?

DOCTOR: Chin up. It won't do your wife - or anyone
             else for that matter - any good for you to
             blame yourself. I'll do more than enough of
             that for all of us once I've sorted this mess
             out.

BROXTON: You really think you can fix this?

DOCTOR: Of course I can - most probably. Well, it's
             likely that I can. Possibly.

BROXTON: That doesn't fill me with confidence.

DOCTOR: Hold on. I think our luck's changing. Up
             ahead.

BROXTON: A police car. Hey. Over here.

The car pulls up, scrunching in the snow.

DOCTOR: Gentlemen, mere words cannot describe how
             delighted we are to see you.

A roar - a T Rex roar.

BROXTON: Save the speeches, Doctor, and get in.

Doors opening and slamming shut. More roaring.

COP: What the...

DOCTOR: Before you ask, yes, that is a Tyrannosaurus Rex which has followed the General and myself through time in an effort to make us its lunch. Now I suggest you drive us away from here as fast as you possibly can without crashing. Now.

BROXTON: Only in New York.

DOCTOR: I knew a T Rex was hard to shake off but this is ridiculous.

10.
New York Subway.
Footsteps echo as Peri's group are led into the subway, which is acting as an emergency camp for the few survivors.

BARKER: Come on in. It's not much but it's home.

PERI: Why bring everybody to a subway station.

BARKER: For some reason the damage isn't so bad underground and we can use the tunnels to move around without being attacked by any of the animals up top.

There is a buzz of low conversation.

PERI: Is this all that's left of New York? How many people are down here?

BARKER: Two hundred and some here. The same in half a dozen other stations. It's not much for a city the size of this. God only knows what happened to the rest.

175

ALAN: You said you had some patients for me.

BARKER: Yeah. We've been trying to find a doctor
             since this started. We tried the hospitals but,
             hell, we found some of the worst cases there.

PERI: Worst cases of what?

BARKER: Over here. I'll show you.

Footsteps echo on platform. Still a low rumble of conversation.
Metal train doors are opened.

BARKER: We keep them on the trains, behind these
             curtains so the rest don't see them.

There are moans and wails - pitiful sounds of extreme pain.

PERI: Oh, God. I feel sick.

BAXTER: (Tired, resigned and more than a little bit
             scared.)
             That's pretty much what I said when I saw
             them.

ALAN: I've never seen anything like it. This man
             looks like he's got concrete growing out of
             his side.

BAXTER: There's worse than him. One woman has a
             light fitting coming out of her face, a kid's
             got an electric socket stuck in his throat.
             Some of them have bits of brick growing out
             of their bodies. And we have dozens more
             like them. Hell, some of them would be
             comical if you didn't see how much pain
             these people are in. We found one guy with
             dinner plates embedded in either side of his
             head. In silhouette he looked like Mickey

	Mouse. At least until he died. Can you do anything for them, doc?
ALAN:	I'm not a surgeon - and even if I was, I don't think I could remove any of the things that are stuck through these people.
BARKER:	Why not?
ALAN:	It wouldn't be like taking a bullet out of a gunshot wound. These things haven't been pushed through those people.
PERI:	It looks more like they're part of them.
CARRA:	The objects and the patients are bonded at a sub-molecular level.
BARKER;	What?
CARRA:	(Puzzled) How do I know this?
BARKER:	Good question. Another one is can you help them?
ALAN:	The best I can do is give them something for the pain. Do you have any anaesthetic?
BARKER:	We had some, but we ran out and we weren't sure what else we could use.
PERI:	If Alan makes a list, you could...
ALAN:	... have some of your people go and collect it. You're beat. How long is it since you had any sleep?

BARKER: I was on a long shift when this hit - maybe thirty hours.

ALAN: I'm prescribing sleep - at least six hours. No arguments.

Sound of the metal train doors closing.

BARKER: You win. Even a nightmare will be light relief after this. There's some food out here on the platform. Pretty basic but it's hot. We even managed to rustle up some blankets and a few cots. Oh, and give your name to Sergeant Kelly - she's the one with the clipboard there. It may not come to anything but we'd like to know who we've got here.

PERI: We'd better come up with a name for you. I don't feel up to explaining the truth.

CARRA: (Thoughtful)
Carra.

PERI: Carra?

CARRA: Yes. I will be called Carra.

ALAN: It's a nice name, but why pick that one?

PERI: The poster on the boards. It's for an album called Cara Mia. You can read.

CARRA: Yes. Why can I read? Why can I say things and make you understand them? And why do I see squiggles that I recognise as letters that make words? Why can I do these things now? Yesterday, I had no language, no thoughts past what to eat and where to sleep. What has happened to me?

PERI: Calm down. You're gonna be okay.

CARRA: How can you know that?

PERI: Because I know the Doctor. He wouldn't have done this to you if he thought it there was any danger to you.

ALAN: You will be okay. I won't let anything bad happen to you.

CARRA: I have already saved your life twice.

ALAN: Exactly. I owe you, and since I hate being in debt, I'll hang around till I can pay you back.

CARRA: Good. I trust you.

PERI: You two go and get some food. I'm going to see if anybody's seen the Doctor. I know it's a long shot but I have to try.

DOCTOR: If anybody has seen me be sure to tell me where I've been.

PERI: Doctor! You're alive.

The Doctor "Ooofs!" a bit. He's obviously getting a severe hug.

DOCTOR: Obviously, though you are making it rather difficult to breathe.

PERI: Sorry. But I thought I'd lost you.

DOCTOR: You don't get rid of me that easily. How's the rest of your little group?

PERI: Alan's tired but okay, and Carra is, well, different.

DOCTOR: Carra? You gave her a name?

PERI: She gave herself a name. Whatever you did, Doctor, you did too much of it. She can speak and read, and she knows something weird has happened to her.

DOCTOR: Oh, dear. I must have augmented her a little more than I intended. We'll think about that later. By the way, this is General Broxton. General, Miss Peri Brown, a very dear friend of mine.

BROXTON: Miss Brown.

PERI: Do you know what happened yet?

DOCTOR: Oh, yes. We know, don't we, General? Now all I have to do is work out some way of putting it right within the next few hours. Simple, really.

PERI: Doctor, only you could say that and sound like you could do it.

DOCTOR: Get your two new friends, Peri. We have to get going. General, you talk to whoever is in charge and see about getting us some transport.

BROXTON: (Sarcastic)
        Yes, sir. And might I ask what you'll be doing?

DOCTOR: Having a cup of soup. I'm feeling rather peckish,. Now off you go, both of you.

(Sniffs appreciatively)
Ah. Manna.

A roar fills the subway.

BARKER: What the hell?

More roars.

BARKER: Open fire. Shoot.

Gunfire.

11.
Scout's Chamber. The Robot is reporting again.

ROBOT: Target has been pursued by T Rex.

SCOUT: Do nothing to interfere. Simply observe.

12.
The subway.
Roars and gunfire.

BROXTON: I thought we'd lost that thing.

DOCTOR: T Rex's rarely give up any pursuit.

PERI: We have to do something.

DOCTOR: Down onto the track, all of you. Head into the
                     tunnel.

BROXTON: Doctor, I am damned if I will run away and
                     leave these people...

DOCTOR: General, you will do as you are told! Now go.
                     I know what I'm doing. Go.

PERI: Alan, Carra. Come on.

DOCTOR: Go. Hurry. Keep going. Right.
(Pause, then he shouts loudly)
Hello? Hello! You with the small brain and
bad breath! I rather think it's me you're after.
Ignorant brute. Hoi! Yoohoo!

BROXTON: What's he doing? Is he crazy?

PERI: Probably.

ALAN: If he wanted that thing's attention, he's got it.

BROXTON: And it's chasing him this way.

DOCTOR: Run!

13.
The subway platform.

BARKER: The guy in the clown suit has drawn it away
down the tunnel.
COP: Brave guy. Even stooped almost double that
animal's fast.

BARKER: Do we still have explosives?

COP: Sure.

BARKER: Set them at the tunnel entrance. There's no
way that monster's coming back in here.

13.
The tunnel.
With roars behind them, the Doctor's crew are still running.

PERI: It's not catching up.

DOCTOR: Unfortunately we'll tire and slow long before
            it does.

The sound of an explosion.

ALAN: What the hell was that?

PERI: They've blown up the tunnel. We can't go
            back.

Episode 4

1.
Recap from part 3.
The subway tunnel.
The T Rex is roaring behind them, and the Doctor's party are scarpering along the tunnel.

PERI: It's not catching up.

DOCTOR: Unfortunately, we'll tire and slow long before it does.

The sound of an explosion.

ALAN: What the Hell was that?

PERI: They've blown up the tunnel. We can't go back.

The T Rex is roaring in discomfort.

BROXTON: The T Rex. The shockwave from the explosion must have disoriented it.

DOCTOR: More likely the noise, but whatever it is, it's given us the time we need. That ladder ahead. Everybody start climbing. Hurry. The T Rex won't be dazed for long.

Sounds of clambering and feet on rungs. The Rex roars again.

PERI: It's spotted us.

DOCTOR: So I see. Keep climbing. After you, my dear.

CARRA: Thank you.

More feet on rungs.

DOCTOR: Hurry up.

CARRA: I can't. Everyone else has stopped climbing.

BROXTON: The grille to street level is frozen shut. I can't get it open.

DOCTOR: You're a military man. Use brute strength - I thought that was what you were supposed to be good at.

ALAN: Here. I'll help.

BROXTON: (Muttering)
              If I live through this, so help me, I swear I'll throttle that man. On three. Push.

ALAN: (Straining)
              It's moving.

PERI: Push again.

The grate scrapes open.

DOCTOR: Everybody up. Hurry.

Footsteps on the rungs. The T Rex roars.

PERI: Doctor, hurry. It's almost on top of you.

DOCTOR: Believe me, I know!

The T Rex roars loudly and the Doctor thumps hard into the snow.

PERI: That was close.

DOCTOR: Nonsense. I had everything timed to the micro-second. More or less.

Iain McLaughlin

T Rex roars.

DOCTOR: (To T Rex)
               Good try, old chap, but bad luck. Have a nice
               day.
               (He drops the grate back into place)
               Missing you already. Now, general, I believe
               you have some plans to throttle me.

BROXTON: Don't tempt me, Doctor. Not even a little bit.

ALAN: Back to the subway station?

DOCTOR: To wait for the world to end? No, we're going
               to a military installation just outside the city.
               It's the best chance we have of putting things
               back on track.

BROXTON: We'd better get started. It's going to be a long
               hike.

DOCTOR: Walk? You expect me to yomp all that way in
               this weather? As dear Noel Coward once said,
               not on your nellie. See if you can find a four
               wheel drive car large enough for all of us.

 ALAN: How about this? It even has the keys in the
               ignition.

DOCTOR: Excellent.

Car door opening.

BROXTON: Where do you think you're going?

DOCTOR: The driver's seat.

BROXTON: You don't know the way. I'll drive.

186

DOCTOR: I am licenced to drive more vehicles in more
            star systems than you can count. I'll drive.

Car door shuts. The engine starts.

PERI: I'm driving. Look, this is my home town and
            I know my way around. Get in.

DOCTOR: Fine.
            (Sounds of him getting in the car, then
            discomfort.)
            What are you doing?

BROXTON: Sitting up front with you two. You need me to
            give directions to the base.

PERI: Give me strength. You two cosy back there?

CARRA: Yes, thank you.

DOCTOR: Good grief.

PERI: See? I told you she'd come a long way.

DOCTOR: I think I may have made a terrible mistake.

PERI: Hold on. This could be bumpy.

The car moves off, bumping and scrunching in the snow.

ALAN: Here. Hold my hand.

CARRA: Why?

ALAN: I don't know. I just thought you might be, you
            know, a bit nervous.

CARRA: No.

ALAN:	Oh.
CARRA:	But if you are feeling nervous, you may hold my hand.
ALAN:	I do get edgy on long car journeys.
CARRA:	In my tribe, when two men fight for a woman, it is because they want her as a mate. I realise that you fought only to protect me. I will not hold you to anything else.
ALAN:	No?
CARRA:	Unless you want me to.
ALAN:	What do you say we hold hands and enjoy the view?

2.
The Scout's chamber.
Another report is coming in from the Robot.

| ROBOT: | Target has escaped the T Rex and is making for the Military Research Centre. |
| SCOUT: | That is unfortunate. He cannot be allowed to interfere. Maintain surveillance. I will signal the Hub-ship to break temporal orbit and prepare to land. |

3.
The car.
The car is jostling and jolting along. It hits a particularly hefty bump, getting varied oofs and yelps.

| PERI: | Sorry. |

DOCTOR: Just as well I didn't manage to have any of that soup. I'm not sure it would have reacted well to all this bumping about.

PERI: Don't blame me. I'm doing the best I can.

DOCTOR: I'm sure you are. Really.

PERI: And anybody who complains can get out and walk. Got it?

BROXTON: Got it.

DOCTOR: Oh, yes. Absolutely. I'm...

The time distortion sound hits very suddenly. The Doctor's speech continues - slowed like a 78 record played at 33. (Showing my age there.)

DOCTOR: ... sure you're doing a fine job.

PERI: (Also slowed)
            Don't...
            (Her voice speeds up. Now it's a 33 played at 78)
            ... patronise me, you chauvenist...
            (Voice returns to normal)
            ...porker.

ALAN: What the hell was that?

CARRA: A time ripple.

DOCTOR: (Surprised)
            Exactly. Time is beginning to come together here for the big explosion. We're almost out of time.

PERI: Where's the snow gone?

BROXTON: It's just rock.

DOCTOR: A primordial plain from before even the first life appeared. A different time is trying to inhabit this space. How much further?

BROXTON: A few miles.

DOCTOR: Peri, I believe the term is, floor it.

Engine guns.

4.
The engine hisses. Now there are sounds of jungle.

PERI: Don't blame me.

DOCTOR: I didn't say a word.

PERI: It wasn't my fault. How was I supposed to know there would be another of those time ripple things? And I certainly couldn't predict it was going to stick a whopping great tree in front of us.

DOCTOR: Exactly.

PERI: I hate it when you're reasonable.

DOCTOR: At least no-one is hurt. Are they?

ALAN: A few bruises but we'll get by.

BROXTON: By my reckoning we're around a quarter of a mile from the research centre.

DOCTOR: A brisk walk will do us the world of good. Come along.

5.
Scout's chamber.
The Robot is reporting again.

ROBOT: The target and his party have reached the
                research centre.

SCOUT: The Hub-ship will arrive in less than a
                minute. Stand by.

6.
Outside the research centre.

BROXTON: Oh, my God.

ALAN: This is the research centre? We came all this
                way for that?

BROXTON: It's ruined.

DOCTOR: The tides of time wait for no man? Don't you
                believe it. I have a feeling that things may not
                be as bad as they first appear. Inside, quickly.

PERI: Doctor, the place is a write-off.

DOCTOR: On the outside, yes. But the General told me
                that his people used exotic matter to create a
                warp field bubble...

7.
Inside the Research Centre.
A slight hum of a warp bubble and working machinery.

DOCTOR: ... which might just have been enough to
                protect the lab where the experiment was
                running.

BROXTON: It's untouched. Everything's working - even the generator. It's down one storey.
(Thinks for a moment.)
Where are my scientists?

DOCTOR: I imagine they ran when the tachyon emissions began.

BROXTON: I ordered them out. They'd have been safe if they stayed here.

DOCTOR: Yes.

PERI: You couldn't have known.

BROXTON: I should have. I should have known every damn possible problem before letting the experiment start.

DOCTOR: We don't have time for your self-pity. Yes, this might work. We can use this little lot to create an inverse temporal wave to counteract the one that's caused this trouble. The energy released when they clash will send everything back to it's proper place in time.

CARRA: Everything?

DOCTOR: I'm afraid so. Yes.

CARRA: I understand.

ALAN: Wait. You mean Carra will have to go back to her own time?

DOCTOR: I'm sorry.

ALAN: No way. You can't...

The building shakes and rumbles.

BROXTON: What the ...?

DOCTOR: It's not the time disruption.

PERI: Doctor. At the door.

ALAN: What the hell is that?

DOCTOR: A surveillance unit of some sort. Can I help
            you at   all?

ROBOT: You cannot be allowed to interfere with time.

DOCTOR: Quite the reverse actually. We're trying to put
            it back on course.

ROBOT: Time must follow its' set path. You cannot be
            allowed to interfere.

DOCTOR: Now listen here...

The sound of a hi-tech weapon and then quiet.

8.
A quiet room. The Doctor groans, coming round.

DOCTOR: ...you tin-plated... Where am I?

PERI: We were hoping you could tell us.

DOCTOR: Metal walls? No furniture? No windows?

DOCTOR & PERI: (Chorus)
            A cell.

BROXTON: (Sarcastic)
            I'd never have guessed.

PERI: Can the sarcasm, okay, and try finding a way
             out.

CARRA: Alan?

ALAN: (Groaning and coming round.)
             Yeah. Yeah, I hear you. Are you okay?

CARRA: Better than you, I think. Get up slowly. You
             will be dizzy for a few seconds.

BROXTON: A little dizziness never hurt anybody. We
             need everybody looking for a way out. Save
             your pillow talk for later.

ALAN: We wouldn't need to look for a way out if
             you hadn't cause this.

BROXTON: And you've been quick enough to exploit it
             with the cave cutie.

CARRA: Leave him alone or I will kill you here.

DOCTOR: ENOUGH! If bickering is the best you can
             manage in this situation then perhaps
             humanity doesn't deserve to survive.

BROXTON: You're right.

A panel in the wall buzzes open.

PERI: I just checked that bit of wall.

DOCTOR: Shush.

The robot hums into view.

DOCTOR: I remember you. You shot us. I don't like
             you.

ROBOT:	You will come with me.
BROXTON:	So you can kill us?
PERI:	If it wanted to kill us, it could have done it any time.
DOCTOR:	Precisely. Shall we?

9.
Spaceship.
The Doctor's party are being marched along a corridor.

ALAN:	This might sound dumb, but this is a spaceship, right?
PERI:	Looks like one.
BROXTON:	Spaceship, my ass.

Hum of another door opening.

SCOUT:	Come in. You will not be harmed.
DOCTOR:	You were saying, General?
BROXTON:	My God, what are those things?
DOCTOR:	I imagine we'll soon find out.
SCOUT:	You have nothing to fear, General Broxton.
BROXTON:	How do you know my name?
SCOUT:	You are the reason we are here.
DOCTOR:	Really? You wouldn't care to explain that, would you?

SCOUT: Who are you?

DOCTOR: Who am I? I am.... nobody important, really.
              Just curious.

SCOUT: Without General Broxton, my race would not
              exist.

BROXTON: Just what is that supposed to mean?

DOCTOR: It's obvious, isn't it?

PERI: Not to us mere mortals.

DOCTOR: Take a look at our little hosts, Peri. Don't
              they look even a little familiar?

PERI: Not really. I've seen a lot of weird stuff since
              I met you but I've never met freaky, four foot
              high grey-skinned aliens with way big heads -
              no offence.

DOCTOR: Look closer. Bipedal. Four finger and a
              thumb on each hand. Five toes per foot. Just
              like humans. You're not aliens at all, are you?

BROXTON: Then who are they?

DOCTOR: They're what humanity will become after this
              disaster. I'm right, aren't I?

SCOUT: Yes. The energy released by the temporal
              explosion tilted the Earth off its' axis. The
              dust and debris from the explosion stayed in
              the atmosphere for decades. Across the Earth,
              less than a hundred thousand humans
              survived.

DOCTOR: And you had to evolve to survive. Larger brains, smaller bodies, that sort of thing.

SCOUT: We have evolved into a wiser, more peaceful race than humanity. That is why we could not let you alter time. If there is no explosion, we will never exist.

ALAN: But billions of people will die.

SCOUT: They will die because they have always died. It is history.

DOCTOR: What if I told you that I have seen future - and I know that Earth was not destroyed in 1985? That billions of people did not die in a global catastrophe? That there was no global catastrophe for them to die in?

SCOUT: You are lying.

PERI: He's not!

DOCTOR: If you examine me, you will find that despite appearances I am not human.

SCOUT: Scans confirm your statement. It is of no consequence. We must survive.

DOCTOR: Listen, I know this is difficult for you to accept, but you must believe me when I say, that you should not exist. Your species is a most unfortunate consequence of a rift in time which must be put right.

SCOUT: Your statement will be examined.

DOCTOR: Good.

SCOUT: After the explosion has occurred.

DOCTOR: Haven't you listened to a word I've said?

SCOUT: There will be no more discussion. You may
              watch the explosion here, or you may wait in
              your chamber. Afterwards, you can be
              released here unharmed, or you may return to
              the future with us.

PERI: That's big of you.

ALAN: I can't watch it.

PERI: Nor me.

DOCTOR: I don't think any of us can. General...

BROXTON: I'm staying.

DOCTOR: That isn't a good idea.

BROXTON: I'm staying. I started this. I'll see the end.

DOCTOR: Listen to me. Your time would be better
              served elsewhere.

BROXTON: (Realising something's brewing)
              It would? Okay.

SCOUT: You will be escorted to your chamber. We
              will tell you when it is done.

DOCTOR: How long?

SCOUT: Eight minutes.

ROBOT: Follow me.

10.
Spaceship.
The Doctor's crew are heading for their chamber.

PERI: Whatever you're planning, Doctor, you'd better be quick. We only have a few minutes.

DOCTOR: We have to lose the tour-guide first. Excuse me. Isn't this our room?

Door opening.

ROBOT: No. That is restricted. Close door at once.

Door begins to close.

DOCTOR: Got you.

ROBOT: Release me...

Door crunches on metal.

ROBOT: Rel...

Nothing. The Robot is dead.

ALAN: Where did you learn to catch like that?

DOCTOR: I used to be a top-class slip fielder.

BROXTON: Which way out?

DOCTOR: At a guess, this way.

They hurry away.

11.
Spaceship.
The group are hurrying.

BROXTON: That looks like a hatch.

CARRA: Wait.

BROXTON: We don't...

CARRA: Something is coming. I hear it.

PERI: There. It's one of those grey people.

SCOUT 2:   You should not be here. You...

The sound of a solid punch.

BROXTON: Problem solved.

ALAN: Permanently. It's dead.

BROXTON: I didn't hit it that hard...

ALAN: Hard enough.

DOCTOR: That was unnecessary. If you ever do that
              again, I may just leave you and your
              miserable planet to rot. Do I make myself
              clear?

BROXTON: And if you don't get this hatch open, billions
              of people will die in less than five minutes.
              Do I make myself clear?

Spark, flash and the door hums open.

PERI: What are we waiting for?

12.
Ship's control room.
An alarm sounds.

COMPUTER: Prisoners have escaped.

SCOUT: Show me. They have killed one of us. Prepare ship for lift-off. Ready the weapons. They will not stop history.

13.
Research Centre.
The Doctor's party run in.

DOCTOR: Excellent. They didn't deactivate the machinery.

BROXTON: Rigg, you and Captain Cavewoman make yourself useful and barricade the door.

ALAN: Yes, Sir, General sir.

CARRA: This desk is not important. We can use it.

DOCTOR: Calibrate the field generator...

PERI: Doctor...

DOCTOR: Shush. I'm busy.

A bit of a low, rumbling hum.

BROXTON: Doctor...

DOCTOR: What is it? This isn't like programming a video recorder. It takes absolute concentration.

An explosion shakes the centre.

ALAN: That explosion was nothing to do with time.

CARRA: They have discovered that we have escaped.

Another explosion.

PERI: And they're not too happy.

CARRA: For every creature, the will to survive is
               strong.

BROXTON: You'd better hurry it up, Doctor.

DOCTOR: I am doing my best, you know. It isn't easy,
               particularly with this primitive set-up of
               yours.

BROXTON: That primitive set-up cost over three billion
               tax dollars.

DOCTOR: Ludicrous. Wasting your money on folly like
               this when you could have used it to feed the
               starving, build hospitals, educate children...

Another explosion. Closer, this time.

CARRA: That was closer.

PERI: Those were our warning shots. Next time, it'll
               be for real.

BROXTON: Doctor, we're out of...

DOCTOR: Finished. It's set.

BROXTON: Do it.

Nothing.

BROXTON: Do it.

PERI: What are you waiting for?

ON THE SHELF

DOCTOR: I can't do it.

BROXTON: What?

DOCTOR: If I engage the inverse temporal wave, the
            spaceship above us, its' occupants and all of
            their kind who would ever live will blink out
            of existence. They will never have the chance
            to exist.

PERI: And if you don't, billions of humans who you
            know should live won't get that chance.

DOCTOR: Either way it's genocide. I don't have the
            right to make a decision on that scale. No-one
            does.

BROXTON: If you won't start this thing, I will. Get out of
            my way.

Another explosion, this one, taking the door off the hinges (not
that we see it.)

CARRA: The door is gone.

PERI: Doctor, you have to decide. It's them or
            humanity.

DOCTOR: Or is it? Perhaps I have to choose a third
            option.

BROXTON: What third option is there?

DOCTOR: Peri, get the cover off that control panel.
            Breaking every law of time known to man or
            Time Lord, General. I'm going to use the
            release of energy to split the future so that
            both of these possible futures can and do
            happen.

ALAN: Is that possible?

DOCTOR: No, I'm just doing this to while away the few
                 remaining seconds before the world blows up.

PERI: Of course it's possible. Isn't it?

DOCTOR: Just recalibrate the frequency to match the
                 one I'm sending.

PERI: How do I do that?

CARRA: The reading top left. Use the key-pad just
                 below it. Am I correct?

DOCTOR: (Surprised)
                 Exactly.

Another explosion, again closer.

CARRA: I think something is moving out there.

ALAN: Don't. Come back...

The rumble of a roof falling in.

PERI: Look out. The roof.

ALAN: Help me shift this. There.

PERI: Is she alive?

ALAN: The doorway took most of the hit but we need
                 to get her out from under this. Help us.

BROXTON: She'll have to wait. Doctor, is everything still
                 operational?

DOCTOR: Just checking. Yes.

BROXTON: Start it.

DOCTOR: You're a true humanitarian. Peri, Doctor
               Rigg. Over here, please.

ALAN: We can't leave her like this. She'll be outside
               the protection of the warp bubble.

DOCTOR: I know.

PERI: What?

DOCTOR: This isn't her time. She has to go back to her
               own place in space and time. If she doesn't
               there could be side-effects.

ALAN: I don't give a damn about any side-effects. I
               care about her.

CARRA: The Doctor is correct. I must go back. Go
               inside.

ALAN: I'm staying.

BROXTON: Damn fool.

DOCTOR: You think so?

BROXTON: Doctor, get back here.

PERI: Doctor?

DOCTOR: I've a feeling I'm going to regret this. Peri,
               you be ready to pull Carra free when we lift
               this. Ready.

ALAN: Ready.

DOCTOR: Lift.

ALAN: It's not moving.

DOCTOR: Try man, we're almost out of time.

Strained grunts and moans.

BROXTON: This is my centre. If anybody's moving
               anything, it's me.

DOCTOR: Good man. Put your shoulder to it.

The rubble scrapes and moves.

DOCTOR: Now, Peri. Pull.

PERI: Got her.

DOCTOR: Get her inside. Quickly.

Another explosion. More rubble falls.

BROXTON: Now, Doctor.

ROBOT: Step away from the machine or you will be
               killed.

DOCTOR: Doesn't your type of robot ever say anything
               interesting?

ROBOT: Step away from the machine or you will be...

DOCTOR: Apparently not. Goodbye.

14.
Spaceship.

SCOUT: Kill him. Don't let him...

15.

Time effect. Waves and swirls of the distortion. Bits of dialogue from the characters through the story can just about be heard and recognised as voices but what they're saying isn't clear. It builds to a wild crescendo then stops abruptly.

16.
Spaceship.

SCOUT: The explosion occurred as history dictated. We are safe.

17.
Research Centre.
The original accident is just about to happen. The distortion sound is building again.

SCIENTIST: It's out of control. It's giving out types of radiation I've never seen before. I don't know what's happening here. General, do something. It's out of control. It's going to...

BROXTON: Get out of the way. Doctor? It's happening again.

DOCTOR: Excuse me. Move. Reverse the flux matrix's polarity and feed it back through the build up of the wave ...

Sound dies down.

DOCTOR: And that should take care of it.

SCIENTIST: It's gone. How did you do that?

DOCTOR: That? Oh, it was nothing, really. And that's all I'm telling you.

PERI: It's safe now?

DOCTOR:	Totally.
BROXTON:	My wife? Everybody in the city?
DOCTOR:	Safe. Doing whatever they were doing before... nothing happened.
SCIENTIST:	General, who are these people? Where...?
BROXTON:	That's... classified. I want you to collate all the information on this experiment.
SCIENTIST:	We know the drill, General.
BROXTON:	After Christmas, and then we shut this project down permanently.
SCIENTIST:	General?
BROXTON:	Go home. See your families.
DOCTOR:	That is, if I may say, very wise. Time really shouldn't be tampered with.
BROXTON:	What do you call her?
CARRA:	You should have let me go back to my own time.
DOCTOR:	More than likely, young lady. There'll probably be some side-effects from you being out of synch with time.
CARRA:	Why didn't you leave me?
ALAN:	Not that we're complaining.
DOCTOR:	I made the mistake of augmenting your mind too much. I was in a hurry. If I'd had the time

I could have removed the knowledge I gave you - but you'd have known something was wrong. And to send you back to a primitive time as you are now? That would have been cruel. You don't belong there anymore.

BROXTON: So you changed time, just like you lectured me for doing. You're a hypocrite, Doctor.

DOCTOR: Probably. I've been called worse.
PERI: Actually, I think you're a romantic. They do make a cute couple.

DOCTOR: Do they? I suppose.

Out-of-breath marine charges in.

MARINE: General. Sir it's...

BROXTON: What is it? Let's hear it.

MARINE: I.. I... I'll show you.

18.
Research Centre. Exterior.
There are quiet trumpetings and sounds of Mammoths.

MARINE: They just... appeared.

PERI: I think we've found the side-effect, Doctor. A whole herd of them.

BROXTON: What in hell am I going to do with them?

DOCTOR: I'd suggest feeding them. Your grounds don't have enough greenery to support thirty five, no, over forty Woolly Mammoths for long. And I'm sure they wouldn't say no to a nice drink of water.

BROXTON: What do I know about Mammoths?

PERI: Ask Carra - she's seen them all her life. She
             could really help you study them.

DOCTOR: And put them somewhere safe and far away
             from prying eyes. Ironic, isn't it? You almost
             destroy humanity, and wind up by giving a
             fresh chance of life to a noble species wiped
             out by humanity, Look after them.

BROXTON: I will.

DOCTOR: And you two... at least put each other down
             long enough to listen to my pearls of wisdom.

ALAN: Sorry. It's just... you know.

DOCTOR: Actually, no I don't.

PERI: Or if he does he's not owning up to it.

DOCTOR: If you two are going to be together it's going
             to be difficult for you. Particularly you, Carra.
             You may regret staying here, but you're stuck
             with it. Muddle on as best you can. I think
             you'll be fine.

CARRA   Will I continue to get smarter?

DOCTOR: Er, no. Whatever I put in your mind you
             know by now. In fact, you'll probably start
             forgetting things, but no more so than any
             normal person.

CARRA: Thank you. For showing me this.

ALAN: Double for me. I don't think I'll work
             Christmas this year after all.

DOCTOR: Of course, you're probably both mad, but
            you'll be happy together.

PERI: You've saved the world, brought a species
            back from the dead and played cupid.

DOCTOR: I suppose I have been a tad busy.

PERI: So there's only one thing left now.

DOCTOR: Which is?

PERI: Getting me home to see my mother? Or had
            you forgotten that's why we came here to
            begin with?

DOCTOR: I don't need an aid memoire just yet. Let's
            see if we can cadge a lift into town. Mind
            you, I've no idea how we're going to explain
            my change in appearance to Harold.

PERI: Howard. And we'll think of something. Hey.
            Would you believe it? It's starting to snow. I
            think we're gonna get a white Christmas.

The Mammoths snort a little and the Doctor harrumphs.

Notes

This script was sent to Big Finish in 2000 along with *The Lone Warrior* and *The Eye of the Scorpion*. Gary Russell returned it with *The Lone Warrior* but he kept *Scorpion* and after a number of rewrites, *Scorpy* got the go-ahead.

What did *Eye of the Scorpion* have that this one didn't?

Frankly, I think Erimem was a big part of *Scorpy* making it to production. I also think there's an energy in that story that's missing in *A Stitch in Time*. I don't think *A Stitch in Time* is actually a bad story. In fact, quite the opposite. There's a lot in it that I do like. The idea of smashing times together in interesting, and I like the horror aspect of people being mashed together with objects – like the person who has plates stuck in his head making him look like Mickey Mouse. I think the Doctor enhancing cave-girl Carra's mental abilities is an interesting idea, but one I didn't write particularly well. In retrospect there should have been more internal conflict in her as all of the new information in her battled with the lifetime of instinct and experience she had. I made it too glib and easy, and focused on the unlikely romance rather than on the conflict in Carra herself. I also didn't look at all into how she would feel about the life she had left behind. It's quite arrogant to assume that she would prefer living in contemporary times to living in her own times. I very much like her as a character and I like the relationship she has with Alan, but I should have written it better.

I think Carra became very passive in the story, too. That was another flaw that came out of focusing on the relationship with Alan. Her instincts should had made her far more pro-active and dangerous. If I could have mixed all of this with her choosing Alan as her mate, I think she would have been a far more interesting character.

The future-human threat should also have been handled better. It feels bolted on, as if it has been added from a completely different story. I think that's the poorest part of the story. The idea behind it was that the characters should be in enormous jeopardy with the future of the world and all of humanity hanging in the balance... and then, as the heroes think they have started to find a possible answer to their problems, another apparently insurmountable obstacle gets in their way.

It doesn't work.

I had intended that the story would have the feel of a Hollywood disaster movie – the kind you would find Irwin Allen's name on. Unfortunately, I think I may have been a bit too accurate with that. Often in those, a threat arrives at the last minute out of nowhere, just because the tension needs ratcheted up a bit. That is how the introduction of the future humans feels to me. They are there for the sake of tension, rather than for the sake of the story, and that is a failure on my part as the writer.

In retrospect, there are two easy ways I could have dealt with the problem. I could have simply removed them and made the journey back to the base more difficult, perhaps giving it more of an *Indiana Jones Meets Jurassic Park* feel. The other alternative would have been to introduce the evolved-humans earlier and to have made more of them all through the story, keeping them as a constant threat floating in the background. Alfred Hitchcock gave an interview about tension. He talked about two men talking at a table. After a minute, the table blows up. There's a shock but there's no tension leading up to it. On the other hand, he pointed out that if you had an establishing shot of the two men talking and then cut to the explosive device under the table, and showed its clock ticking down, and you cut cleverly between the conversation, the people around them and the bomb nearing detonation, you could build unbearable tension. If I had paid attention to Hitchcock and weaved those future humans more wisely through the whole story, they would have been far more interesting and a far greater threat than they were.

General Broxton is also part of the story I would, in retrospect, like to have changed. *Doctor Who* has a history of military commanders who don't act reasonably. General Cutler in *The Tenth Planet* is one who immediately springs to mind. I wanted to make Broxton a bit more three dimensional than some of those military men, but I don't think I achieved that at all. I think a large part of the problem was that the Sixth Doctor is a very confrontational character. He would meet a brash soldier head on, and while I tried to make some of that relationship quite playful, I didn't achieve what I should have. It's a lesson I have learned from, and since writing *A Stitch in Time*, I am always much more careful when writing military men that I don't fall into writing a clichéd martinet.

I think some parts of *A Stitch in Time* hold up well enough. Peri gets to lead her little group, and I do think she comes out of it quite strongly. Her relationship with the Doctor is far friendlier than onscreen in Season 22. I like Colin Baker and Nicola Bryant. They're both very gifted performers. I just think they were ill-served by the scripts they had in their time together on Doctor Who. I also think their costumes were appalling. They both deserved better and at Big Finish they have shown how their characters *could* have been. Colin's Doctor is far more engaging and *Doctor-ish* in his audios. When he is given the chance to play a more complex and layered Doctor, Colin Baker always delivers on audio. Similarly, Nicola Bryant has flourished as Peri on audio. Freed from hours of endless bickering and being lusted after, the audio Peri is a more interesting character. With more of a character to work with, Nicola Bryant has done wonders with Peri. When I was doing rewrites on *The Eye of the Scorpion*, producer and director Gary Russell told me to keep Peri strong, and not to make her weak, a screamer or a victim. That is something that has stuck with me. I always has a strong female protagonist in stories. I know there are some people who dislike that thinking. There are people who have complained about the 2015 *Mad Max* and *Star Wars* films having strong females in leading roles. Frankly, if you've got a problem with strong women in fiction, you're going to have a problem in life. Get over it.

Some aspects of this story may seem familiar. I'm a huge admirer of Edgar Rice Burroughs. I read his books voraciously as a child. I still have a shelf full of his books here in my study. The big cave-man who lusted after Carra in this was very much influenced by Jubal the Ugly One in the first of the *Pellucidar* novels, *At The Earth's Core*. That was in the story as a definite nod to the works of Burroughs and the Amicus films based on them that I loved in the 1970s.

The idea of eras of time crashing together was something that resurfaced when Claire Bartlett and I wrote *Time Heals* the first of Big Finish's *UNIT* series of plays. That story was not in any way an adaptation of this script. We made the temporal distortion far more localized and less threatening to the world in general. *Time Heals* was an action thriller whereas *A Stitch in Time* was a sci-fi disaster movie. The time distortion was far less important and therefore was a much smaller deal in the finished play. However, in the interests of truth I do have to admit that I lifted the basic idea from A Stitch in Time before tweaking it and downscaling it.

The cliffhanger of the first episode has a bit of ghastly writing that makes me cringe. It shouldn't. I had never had any feedback about writing audio drama, and so I didn't think twice about putting in this clunky bit of dialogue.

> PERI: *There. Over the square.*
> ALAN: *It's like a whirlpool of electricity.*

Radio drama needs explanation. You have to tell the listener where people are and what is happening there. Those two lines are a prime example of how *NOT* to do it. Never have people standing still explaining what they're looking at to other people who are there looking at the same thing. It sounds awful when you do. *Really* awful... as those two lines show. How would I have done it now? I'd have asked for violent sounding crackling electric sound effects.

> PERI: *That can't be good.*
> DOCTOR: *It isn't. It's a rip in space time. Keep*
>   *clear of those energy tendrils or they'll*
>   *fry you where you stand.*

That gives a bit of personality to getting more or less the same information across.

There are many other flaws in *A Stitch in Time*, including having a Donald Trump gag in it – I'd replace him with Bill Gates. I'd rather not give Trump any publicity. Or indeed oxygen. It was the second audio play I wrote, and I wrote it without having had any feedback on the first. For example, one of the thing I had never considered was that if I finished one scene with Peri speaking, I shouldn't start the next with Peri speaking unless I was giving some sort of audio cue or bridge to show that we had moved to a different scene. Having characters appear for a single scene also screams out that I didn't know what I was doing. When you're just writing for the sake of writing, you don't think of simple but important questions like "Who's going to play the character?". The first scene of the play has a nurse in it. Who's going to play her? There are only two female characters in the story – Peri and Carra. If either of them played the nurse, it would be spotted. There's no way to justify the expense of bringing in a performer for one scene. So who's going to play her? Likewise, Jacob the Dutch settler in episode three. What do they bring to the play? Who's going to play them? Are they necessary? Can I tell the story just as well without them? That's the kind of thing you start to think about after you've had the experience of writing an audio. The creative side is great, but you have to think of the logistics as well.

Who will play that two-line character?
How do we bridge scenes?
How can the sound engineer make that work?

In retrospect, I'd have made the nurse male or turned him into an orderly. It's rather stereotyping to assume that the nurse would be female anyway – but I did write the character as female, so I am guilty there. If he was male he could have been played with a different accent by one of the actors playing smaller parts later in the play, or by whoever provided the grunts for the big, horny cave man out to bellow sweet nothings in Carra's ear. He was an accidental discovery I've used a few times since – a character who can't actually speak can be very useful on audio. He can grunt and other people talk to or react to him… so you can have a conversation that uses only one actor. I felt so smug when I realized that. And then I found out it was a trick people had been using for years.

However, it's interesting for me to look back at this story, sixteen years after writing it and to see both the failure and the parts of it that still stand up to scrutiny.

Time Heals
All Things

A reworking of *A Stitch in Time* as a potential submission to BBV as a possibility for their single CD *Doctor Who* universe series of audio plays.

Iain McLaughlin

218

Alan Rigg is a doctor in a London hospital. He's 30-something and his life's in a rut. He spends too much time at the hospital and not enough time living a proper life. He knows he's in a rut but doesn't see a way out of it. It's a couple of days before Christmas and he's probably going to volunteer for the Christmas shift again – he's the only doctor in the department who has no wife/partner/family/cute pet to worry about. Tonight, he's supposed to be covering for a friend, but gets the night off when the pal's romantic plans are cancelled.

In a military research facility just outside London, Professor Joe Pernell's working on an experiment into matter transportation. (Though it's never mentioned by name, it's inferred that this may be a descendant of the TOMTIT experiments). In charge of the whole shebang (technical term) is General Carver. He's an upright military sort. Pernell thinks that they should wait. The matter transportation device needs more work, the calculations need to go through the computers again… the whole thing's just not 100% ready yet. But Carver's insistent. He wants the experiment done before Christmas. Pernell starts it up. The computers map the size and composition of a block of lead and prepare to transfer it from one to chamber to another just across the lab by warping space/time and using warp bubbles. It all goes well to begin with but a few moments in, things start to go pear-shaped (another technical term). The warp bubble around the lead block destabilises and loses integrity. The experiment is a failure. Carver slinks off to his office to report the experiment's failure back to the top wallahs at Number 10. While making his call, he gets a report from a frantic Pernell. Something's gone seriously wrong. There's a huge build-up of energy in the lab around the matter transporter device. It's out of control. They can't shut it down. The build-up continues until the sound engulfs the screams of the scientists and a second later, it engulfs Carver as well.

Alan is driving home through London, cursing the Christmas traffic and the Christmas shoppers. He just wants to get home. And then he hears a strange sound coming, getting louder. And then he sees a wild wave of energy coming at him. He swerves his car, losing control and crashing through a shop window as the energy engulfs him as well.

Somewhere out in the open, a woman is running. She is terrified but can't speak. Behind her, there is the roar of a man who sounds more beast than man. She's terrified of him – but she's also terrified of the sound effect that engulfs her.

Alan comes around in the wreckage of his crashed car. He calls for help but none comes so he has to free himself. When he gets out of the car, he realises that something is badly wrong. Outside, there is a blizzard blowing. Nothing unusual in that – it's December after all, but the city seems to have been uncased in ice. Permafrost and glaciers are all around, as though the city has been frozen for decades. He can barely see through the snowstorm but wanders and calls for a while. No joy. As far as Alan can tell, he's the only person left in London.

Pernell wakes up – he was inside the main chamber of the experiment when it all went wonky. The lab is a mess. It sounds old and damp and abandoned, as though hundreds of years have passed since it was used in any way. Pernell is alone. There is nobody else in the lab at all. On further exploration, he finds that there's nobody in the building, not even Carver.

Carver, meanwhile, wakes up in the middle of a jungle, lost and out of sorts.

Alan's trudging through the snowy streets of London (thankfully not singing any Ralph McTell ditties). He hears a trumpeting sound and sees, much to his understandable surprise, a herd of woolly mammoths toddling along past a local branch of Woolworths. He finds that one of the mammoths has stayed behind and is terrorising a young woman, who we'll call Cara (because she'll need a name and it'll be explained later). He manages to distract the mammoth and it slopes off, in search of something more fun to do. Cara is dressed in skins. She's a cave-woman (for want of a better, more technical term). Her bare feet are cut and bleeding from standing in broken glass in a smashed doorway, while trying to keep away from the mammoth. Naturally, she has no idea what glass is. Alan manages to calm her down and inspects her cut feet. She's been lucky. The cuts aren't deep but she will need to have them tended and dressed. The skins she's wearing won't keep her warm either. They need shelter, warmth, first aid equipment and clothing. Cara is a bit nervous about Alan until she hears a roar in the distance. She sticks close to him after that.

Pernell heads out of the research facility and finds himself in what approximates hell on Earth. Thunder, rain, dead ground. There's no sign of life anywhere nearby. He begins trudging along with no idea of where he's going. It doesn't really matter to him. He knows he's destroyed the world.

Alan and Cara are looking for shelter. Most of the buildings are inside glaciers and of no use. Cara's need for shelter is becoming extreme. She is shivering. Alan spots a shopping centre that's not too badly affected by ice. They are heading in when they are attacked by someone from Cara's own time. And he's huge. And vicious. And bad tempered. Oh, and he obviously has a severe case of the horn for Cara, which she's not keen on, all things considered. There's a fight, in which Alan comes out on top by slamming open a car door into his opponent's head. He only wins because he knows what everything around is. Had it been a fair fight, one on one, Alan would have been lucky to get out of it better than dead. As it is, he cheats his way to a win. Too much time watching the WWF. Cara joins in, walloping her would-be suitor with a fallen street sign. The giant caveman is unconscious in the snow – but Alan can't leave him like that. If he leaves him in the snow, the caveman will die. He heaves and shoves the caveman into a car (the one whose door he used to whang the caveman into unconsciousness) and then he and Cara head off. She's thoroughly bemused by his actions but she sticks with him anyway – even closer now. And now they really do need to get into shelter.

Pernell is making his way across the dead landscape when he sees something extraordinary – this must be his day for it. It'll be an interesting page in his diary if he ever manages to get back to his diary. He begins pushing through foliage.

In the jungle, General Carver is having no better a time of it. He hears a chittering sort of sound. Something is moving in the bushes near him. He is getting ready to attack it when Pernell bursts out of the foliage. Their reunion is more one of relief than friendship. Neither really knows what's what. And then they become aware that there really is something in the foliage – lots of somethings. Pack-hunting carnivore dinosaurs. Not velociraptor sized – small and nasty ones. They're timid for now but Carver and Pernell agree that the best course of action is be get as far from these little perishers as possible. As they go, they catch sight of the dinosaurs following them. And then the air by Pernell is disturbed – almost like a mild, very local breeze, only... well, different somehow. As if something passed, but it didn't because they didn't see anything. But they do see the little dinosaurs keeping track of them, albeit at a safe distance.

A computerised voice reports that the target has been found and a humn-ish voice speaks back to the computer, telling it not to interfere but to keep track of the subject.

Alan and Cara are inside a shopping centre. He has happily raided just about every shop in the place for food, first aid and clothes. They have taken camping supplies into a furniture shop where he's got running water to clean her wounds. Her language is very basic – at least he assumes it is because he can't understand a word of it. She's sat on the edge of a bath while he tends to her feet. And he notices that she whiffs a bit. Not her fault. Any caveperson would pong a bit, especially if they hadn't changed their clothes in 10,000 years, but he is worried that she might pick up an infection from the dirt or from her skins outfit. So she has her first bath, which leaves Alan as wet as she is. But at least she's clean, her wounds are treated and she's got warm clothes to wear – although she has real bother with footwear. (A few laughs here, hopefully.)

Carver and Pernell are still yomping through a field. They have a strange experience, looping through a five second period two or three times. (These "wobbles" in time might happen again once or twice later.) Pernell's no expert but he's formulating an idea about what happened. When they attempted to warp space, they ignored the effects it would have on time. As such, they've been bounced back through time. Carver's sure he's never heard so much nonsense in all his life – and he's in touch with parliament so he's an expert on gibberish. Nope, he's not buying that. So how does he explain the little creatures following them? He doesn't – yet. He's more interested in getting away from them. And again, they're buzzed by something in the air. Something they can't see. It must just be the wind playing tricks. And something's making the little dinosaurs skittish.

Alan and Cara are settling around a camp stove when they hear something in the shop – a sabre-toothed cat. They escape by using an old door to slide down an ice-covered staircase.

Alan and Cara have made it to the hospital he works at. They find that they're no the only people alive in the city at all. A couple of patients were left in the hospital and are about to be driven off by the nurse Alan spoke to earlier. Of the several thousand people who should be in the hospital, only these few are left. But the nurse is delighted to see Alan. And a bit surprised that he's got a girl in tow. Unfortunately, the nurse is in no condition to drive. She's dying. As with the patients, she seems to have bits of concrete, plants, plates... you name it, embedded in her. Actually, not embedded – the concrete and other things are almost growing out of them. It happened when that weird storm hit. The nurse lapses into unconsciousness after letting Alan know about a shelter in the subways. They drive off through the snow in an ambulance full of the injured and dying.

Somewhere and somewhen else (that sounds awful doesn't it?) Carver and Pernell are still being followed by the little dinosaurs, who are looking a bit ominous. Not to mention hungry. And then they look skittish. With good reason. A giant roar brings a T Rex into view where it scoffs a couple of the little dinosaurs. Crashing into thicker undergrowth, Carver and Pernell find themselves tumbling down a steep incline to land in a snowdrift. Nearby, is a road with an empty car on it – Carver recognises the road, despite the heavy coating of snow. They're in London. They break into the car and are about to drive off when the T Rex thunders down the incline. It's not happy. It doesn't like the cold but it's not keen on letting them, escape either. It's a hunter and they are on the menu. So it follows the car, which creeps away at a snails' pace.

The ambulance is also creeping through the snow. Eventually they arrive at the Underground and get the patients inside. It's like a scene from WW2. People gathering underground to see out the disaster. Alan is welcomed – there are a lot of people who have been so badly affected with things embedded in or apparently growing out of them. There's not a lot he can do for them except ask for the able folks to go out and get what drugs they can from the shops so that he can at least ease the pain. Around now he gives Cara her name – he has to call her something. He sees a poster for Cara Mia – new operatic album by Pav or one of the other tenors. It's as good as anything. It'll do. She tries to say her name without much success. They settle down to rest. She sits close to him – and he clicks what's happened. He fought with the Giant Haystacks lookalike and in her eyes that means he's picked her as his mate. He's not up for trying to explain things to her at the minute. Besides, he's coming to be rather fond of her.

Two snowy figures enter the subway. A soldier and a man in civvies: Carver and Pernell. They saw the ambulance and came inside. Carver is worried about his wife, who was in London. Pernell is distraught at the suffering their experiment has caused. He has it worked out. They haven't been pushed back through time – time has been scrunched together. Various time periods have been forced together by the experiment. The people who were in the city will be scattered through time or maybe in some kind of limbo between times. And its their fault – his and Carver's. Alan hears him blame himself and pushes for some answers – finally Pernell owns up, despite Carver's complaints that it's a matter of national security. How much does security matter when the world is so screwed? Pernell thinks long and hard and has a notion that there may be a chance to put everything back in place – if the machinery isn't too badly damaged. He's got a theory that the machinery inside the centre of the lab was protected somehow. That's decided. They're heading back to the lab. Carver tries to stop Alan and Cara from joining them but the T Rex, cold, on the verge of collapse and disoriented crashes in. They escape into the train tunnels and climb out through a service ladder. They pile into the ambulance and drive off. They're not happy at abandoning the people in the subway but they don't have weapons – and the best way to save everybody's lives would be to sort things out. Pernell is convinced that rime has become confused by the matter experiments. If he puts it right, everybody goes back to normal.

The observers aren't too happy about this. They don't want to actually kill anybody but they don't want them going back to the lab either. They get ready to move.

The ambulance is having trouble with the terrain but eventually makes it back to the lab – which is a mess. Worse than that – it's a near total write-off. A lot of work will need to be done to get anything to work again, but they might manage it. The warp bubble around the block seems to have extended far enough to protect the lab's generators. Pernell has a plan – or at least a vague idea about putting things back to the way they were. It will need a load of the lab's gear to be working. A lot of the connections are knackered but they can be replaced. This can probably be done.

And the unseen observers really don't like that. Now they do want these people stopped.

And so, while our crew are busy, getting the lab ready, Cara senses something. She can't talk properly (barely at all) but she gets the message over that something's coming. But it's too late. A robot of some kind hovers into view and shoots them with an energy weapon.

When they wake up they are inside a ship of some kind. Their observers are small and humanoid. Actually, they look very human but smaller and frailer and just a bit different. Fact is, they are human – or at least the race humanity evolves into after this catastrophe, which will ultimately wipe out over 99% of the world's population. To survive, the remaining few evolved into these creatures, who now have a population of over 15 million. They have travelled back in time to stop Carver and Pernell from changing things. If the time explosion from the lab didn't happen, this race would never exist. They're not going to stop it now.

Alan's crew are being returned to their cell but Carver engineers an escape. They get out of the ship and back to the lab. The lab comes under attack from the ship but Pernell's busy and they get the lab ready to go. If this works, everybody goes back to their proper place in space and time. Alan's fine with this till he realises that Cara will be bumped back to however many thousand years ago she came from. He's not keen on this. She wants to stay with him as well (as best as she can communicate). Whoever is inside the warp bubble will be safe in the 21st century and Carver's ready to shove Cara out – but Pernell says that it doesn't matter. He's not going through with it. What gives him the right to do this? Who's to say that this isn't how things are meant to be? He's already wiped out one species – he won't do it again. Alan understands, although Carver doesn't. He's only interested in here and now – and in saving humanity. The argument rages – and Alan activates the equipment, knowing that despite being a doctor, he's not only killing these creatures – he's stopping them from ever existing.

And the reset button is hit. The experiment is ongoing. Carver and Pernell are feeling odd. They know something's not right. The experiment? Alan and Cara appear from a side chamber – and it's clear. They remember. They switch off the equipment and close down the experiment. Everything seems to be back to normal but Pernell's sure that there are going to be side-effects of Cara not going back to her own time.

A soldier runs in from outside. It's... well... maybe they should just go outside and see. They go outside and find the grounds are full – of a herd of woolly mammoths. Pernell hasn't wiped out humanity, but he has a chance to be responsible for this great species having a 2nd chance. Alan and Cara... have gone. They've slipped away.

They are at his home, settling in. They've no idea what they're going to do. He gets a call from the hospital asking him to work Christmas. He refuses. He's got other things to do.

Notes

This is a bit of a rarity. After Big Finish decided against A Stitch in Time, I decided to take another look at the story, turning it into a single CD story for BBV without the Doctor or Peri.

For those who don't know who BBV are, they are a company run by Bill Baggs. In the years when Doctor Who was off air after the end of the classic series in 1989, BBV produced videos and then audio plays on CD which were designed to appeal to *Doctor Who* fans. The video films featured the stars of *Doctor Who* in leading roles, and the early releases were very much *Doctor Who* by any other name. Their early audio releases featured Sylvester McCoy and Sophie Aldred as 'the Professor' and his companion 'Ace'. After a complaint from the BBC, the characters were renamed 'Dominie' and 'Alice'. Other releases featured a number of monsters and characters from Doctor Who. These included Zygons, Krynoids, the Rani, Mike Yates and K9. While this story didn't contain any of the monsters, I did think it was possible to tie the story to matter transportation as mentioned in *The Seeds of Death* and *The Time Monster*, which used the wonderfully titled TOMTIT – Transmission Of Matter Through Interstitial Time. It's a tenuous link but BBV weren't averse to stretching things a bit. On top of skating close to the wind with their use of the Doctor himself, they later used the Cyberons in place of the Cybermen. So, I didn't think this was stretching things too badly.

When you have the Doctor in a story, it means you have a classic hero centre stage. He's a strong moral force, brave and resourceful. Taking him out of the story pushed an everyman into the lead role, with Alan becoming the hero. That adds a bit of unpredictability. We always *expect* the Doctor to win. That doesn't diminish the drama in any way. When you've got an eponymous lead character, you always expect them to win out. When you have an everyman hero, there's a chance that no matter how much we like that character, the writer might be enough of a brute to bump him or her off.

Were I ever to go back to the story, I would make a considerable number of changes to it. The first thing would be to work out whether it actually needs both Pernell and Carver. I think the story could have worked just as well with only one of them. It feels overcrowded with both, particularly in the second half. A good question to ask when writing a story is whether you actually need all of the characters you have in there. Often, trimming characters forces you, as a writer, to push your main characters further. Rather than have a scientist who *knows* all the answers, have an everyman who becomes more heroic by *discovering* the solution for himself. What I would do now is have Pernell age to death in front of Carver. They would be friends and Carver would be more driven by having seen his friend die. Restoring his friend to life at the end would be a stronger finale for him than just deciding not to go ahead with the experiment but to have Christmas with his wife instead. Purely as an idea, Christmas with his wife isn't bad, and it does show a human side to him. On the other hand, saving a friend's life – a friend we'd actually meet in the story – is stronger. It's a better use of a character, and will develop Carver more.

Removing Peri and the Doctor would improve Cara's character no end. In the *Doctor Who* version, she's established as a character and then becomes largely a passenger. There's only so much heroic stuff you can fit into a script and the Doctor and his companion get first dibs on it. It's their show. That makes everybody else at best secondary. It's clear Cara would have benefitted enormously from being one of the leads. Her instincts and nature could have been brought more into the plot. Even something simple like knowing how to survive in a blizzard, or how to avoid a predator. Doing that would have elevated her and put her in a place where on occasions Alan is reliant on her. That would make them partners and make their relationship easier to work with. It would also make her far more interesting because she wouldn't have been augmented by the Doctor and what we'd have is her operating with her instincts rather than with an artificial intelligence.

I didn't go far into writing a draft of this version. I didn't see the point in doing an entire draft until it was commissioned. On the other hand, writing a few pages is always useful when you're putting the story together, just to give you a flavor of the characters and how they come to life.

1.

St Peter's Memorial Hospital. London. Day.
It's getting near Christmas. We can hear carol singing in the distance. Dr Alan Rigg (he's 30-ish) is making his weary way through the corridor. There's a drunken belch from a patient.

ALAN   Woah. Careful there, Santa. Too much festive cheer at the office party ? No, I guess not. Nasty. A&E's back that way.

Drunken belch of gratitude.

ALAN   Who'd do a thing like that to Santa? Whoever it is isn't getting any presents this year.

Door opening. Alan yawns mightily.

ALAN   I should have asked Santa for twelve hours' sleep.

He's disturbed by a tinny voice on the PA system.

VOICE   Dr Alan Rigg to the Ward 12. Dr Alan Rigg to Ward 12.

ALAN   I guess I'm not getting it. That's the last time I'm nice to Santa?

2.

Government Military Research Facility. Day.
The Base's CO, General Carver is in conversation with scientist Joe Pernell.

CARVER   Gentlemen, are we ready to begin ?

PERNELL   Well, General, a few more days...

CARVER   A few more days will lead to a few more after that. We've had enough delays on this project. Downing Street is breathing down my neck. They want something in return for the billions of pounds they've ploughed into this enterprise. And more importantly, my wife claims that this project is making me grumpy. Now, I could deal with having to tell Number 10 that we need more time for tests but I don't think I can take another lecture from my wife. Let's give ourselves the best Christmas present we can - and get a positive result for the project. Any objections ?

No answer.

CARVER   That's what I wanted to hear. Let's get this under way.

3.
The hospital.
Alan is yawning. He's approached by Janet, a Welsh nurse.

JANET   Alan ? What are you doing here ? I thought you were off duty three hours ago.

ALAN   You know Kelly ? The nurse in Intensive Care? With the big... hair.

JANET   Big hair. Big prospects. Big chest. You and her?

ALAN   Her and Jon Blake. I'm covering for him.

JANET   Again? And I bet you're working Christmas Day again as well. You spend your time saving lives - maybe you should think about getting on with living one as well.

ALAN   I'm glad you're a good nurse, Janet, coz you're a rotten psychiatrist.

A door slams.

ALAN   Jon ? I thought you and Kelly...

BLAKE   (Not happy)
                She was on call. She had to cover for somebody.
                Go home.

ALAN   Sounds good to me. 'Bye, people.

4.
Military Research Centre.
The machinery is getting cranked up. Carver is still overseeing
things.

CARVER   How long ?

PERNELL   Everything's set... now, General.

CARVER   Good. Hand me that recorder, would you?
                Thanks. December 23rd, 2001. Today, here at
                the Isaac Newton Research Facility , on behalf
                of the British Government, we are about to
                make history. Using strange matter to warp
                space and time, we intend to instantaneously
                transport an object from one sealed chamber,
                through a lead partition to another. If this
                experiment is successful, the technology has
                limitless potential for transporting people, food
                and other resources. The military potential
                should not be overlooked either. General John
                Carver recording.

He switches the recorder off.

CARVER   All recording devices on ?

PERNELL   On.

CARVER   It's time we earned our pay, gentlemen. Begin
                primary power build-up.

The hum of the machinery gets louder.

PERNELL	Rising... fifty percent... seventy five... power levels at optimum.
CARVER	Scan and matt the target block of lead.
PERNELL	Lead block being matted. Dimensions and composition logged in computer.
CARVER	Begin transfer procedure.
PERNELL	Initiating warp bubble around target object. Bubble set and holding.
CARVER	Transfer.

The machinery is louder and then glitches. The steady noise fritzes and crackles. Something is badly wrong.

CARVER	What's wrong ? Why hasn't the block transferred ?
PERNELL	We're losing warp bubble integrity.
CARVER	Hold it steady.
PERNELL	I'm trying, general. I'll try compensating by moving to a lower frequency bandwidth. It's not working. Integrity down to forty six percent. Twenty eight... fifteen... it's gone.

The sound of machinery has died. There is a moment of dead calm - depressed failure.

CARVER	What happened?
PERNELL	I don't know, General.
CARVER	I want every single piece of data relating to this experiment analysed. If we find out what went

wrong here, we can learn from our mistake - and
this won't have been the total failure it looks
like. If anything comes up, I'll be in my office,
reporting to Number 10.

Carver closes a door behind him. We hear him pick up a phone and
punch a number.

CARVER   Get me Under-secretary Lilley at the Ministry of
              Defence.

A slight delay while the call is relayed.

CARVER   Good to hear from you as well, sir. Not good,
              I'm afraid. Well, we're working on that.

There's a buzz from the phone.

CARVER   Would you excuse me for a moment, please,
              Sir?

Beep from the phone as he switches lines.

CARVER   What is it ?

It's Pernell – and he's frantic.

PERNELL   The block of lead - it's emitting tachyon
              particles. We can't stop it. It's building a warp
              field and we can't shut it down. Oh, God, it's
              out of control. It's giving out types of radiation
              we've never seen before. I don't know what's
              happening here.

The sound from the warp bubble is building.

PERNELL   General, we have to do something.

CARVER   Get out of there. Get out of there now!

PERNELL   It's out of control. It's going to...

Pernell's scream is drowned by a strange, screeching explosion.

5.
London.
Alan is driving home. There are honks of horns and the rumble of idling engines in a traffic jam.

ALAN   Come on. Come on. I'd like to get home before
              the New Year arrives. God, I hate Christmas
              traffic.

Honk of horn.

ALAN   And you, arse-face. Why don't you ask Santa
              for a brain this year?

There is a rumbling, screeching sound - the one from the lab - only now it is wilder and getting louder. Horns honk and people begin screaming.

ALAN   Now what ?

The sound - and the screams - get louder.

ALAN   What the hell...?

Screech of tyres as the sound gets louder. Honks his horn.

ALAN   Out of the way. Get out of the damn way.

Crash of glass as he smashes through a plate glass window. The sound gets louder until it overwhelms everything.

6.
Open ground.
Running footsteps. A young woman is gasping for breath as she runs hard. She sounds scared. From behind her comes a roar – wild and uncontrolled, but undeniably human – male. It scares her even more. Even though she's gasping for breath, she runs on.

And then there comes the same sound that affected the research centre and then Alan. The woman leaves scared behind for full-on terrified and screams until the sound cuts off her scream.

7.
Sounds of Alan coming round. His car hisses and he groans. Hollow howling of strong winds outside.

ALAN   God, my head.

Sound of him shoving at the door and trying the handle.

ALAN   Hey. Somebody want to give me a hand here ?
                Hey. Anybody ?

No answer.

ALAN   Never mind. Tell you what. I'll get it myself.
                I'm only stuck in here, but that's okay.

The door finally creaks open with that screeching sound of metal scraping against metal that's almost like fingernails on a blackboard. His feet crunch on broken glass. The wind is howling coldly outside.

ALAN   Where is everybody? Anybody here? God.
                What the hell happened?

He moves through the glass, his feet scrunching it underfoot.

ALAN   Damn glass is a deathtrap.

Now he's outside, the wind is louder.

ALAN   A blizzard? How long was I out? Hello?
                Anybody hear me? Is anybody here? Hello?
                Answer if you hear me! Hello?

No answer. He scrapes at ice and pulls his hand away.

ALAN   Jesus! It's like permafrost. Or a glacier. Hello?

No answer except the wind.

ALAN   Where the hell is everybody?

8.
Int. Research facility lab.
Dripping water. Hollow, echoing . Sounds old and decaying.
Pernell groans. He coughs and struggles for breath.

PERNELL   God almighty. What the hell's happened to this
                place?

It sounds wet and ancient. His feet move through puddles.

PERNELL   Is anybody here?

He pushes a door aside. It scrapes and falls loudly into a puddle of
water.

PERNELL   Hansen? Weaver? Anybody?

More hollow, echoing footsteps.

PERNELL   General Carver?

Pushes a door open. Creaks like it hasn't been opened in centuries.

PERNELL   General? Where are you?

9.
Ext. Jungle.
Sounds of jungle life. Carver wakes up, groggy and out of sorts.

CARVER   What the hell?

10.
Ext London.
The blizzard is still blowing, loud and violent. Alan's footsteps
scrunch in the thick snow.

ALAN   Hello? Anybody?

No answer.

ALAN   (getting a bit desperate)
Hello?

A noise – a sort of trumpeting – very like an elephant only deeper
and louder.

ALAN   What in...

The sound gets louder. Lots of trumpetings and great hairy feet
shuffling through the snow.

ALAN   (shocked – quietly, to himself)
                      Woolly mammoths? I must still be unconscious.

And a yell – female and alarmed. Alan's footsteps pick up speed,
unsteady and slipping in the snow.

ALAN   (optimistic?)
                      Hello?

His footsteps scrunch to a halt. Trumpeting and more yells from
the woman.

ALAN   (quietly, shocked)
                      Jesus.

Louder trumpets and yells.

ALAN   Hey! Leave her alone!

Footsteps digging into the deep snow.

ALAN   Hey. Go on. Go on.

He makes the sort of noises you make to try to distract animals.
Whistles, etc.

ALAN   Hey! Leave her alone. Hey.

The trumpeting changes a little. Sound of something metal being picked up and thrown.

ALAN   Hey.

Trumpeting is louder and more threatening.

ALAN   Yeah. Leave her alone and...

Big, heavy footprints thumping in the snow and trumpeting. It's heading for Alan, who clicks that it's his turn to be in bother now.

ALAN   ...oh, hell.

Sound of him leaping aside and "oofing!" as he lands. The Mammoth thunders by.

ALAN   (quietly, to himself)
                And don't some back.

Parping trumpeting from the mammoth as it toddles off to do whatever mammoths do when they've had enough of terrorising people. Alan's feet scrunch the snow as he gets back to his feet and heads for the woman who yelled.

ALAN   Are you all right?

In return he gets the sounds of someone who is scared and in pain.

ALAN   Your feet are bleeding. Let me see them.

More nervous sounds from the woman. And the sounds of feet moving about in broken glass – more sounds of her being in pain.

ALAN   Don't move around in the glass. You'll make
                your feet worse. You're lucky you haven't
                severed anything major already. Look, I'm not
                going to hurt you. I'm as confused about what
                happened as you are. Let me see your foot.

Quiet whimpers from the woman.

ALAN   The cuts look worse than they are. None of them
                seem to have gone deep but we'd better get you
                away from the glass. This way.

Yelps from the woman, who we'll call Cara (I'll explain later).

CARA   Yamo.

ALAN   I suppose that means you're cold. I 'm not
                surprised. What are you doing out dressed like
                that? The sensible part of my brain says you
                were going to a fancy dress party as queen of
                the cave women. But there's a daft bit of my
                brain that thinks you're something different
                altogether. Unless I imagines that woolly
                mammoth.

Another yelp from Carra.

ALAN   Those feet need dressed. So does the rest of you.
                You need clothes quickly. This way.

Woman grunts and protests.

CARA   Yalu.

ALAN   I'm not going to hurt you. I promise. But you do
                need to get those feet treated.

She's not sure. Then there is a roar - possible human, possibly not.
Whatever, it decides the woman's mind for her. She grunts.

ALAN   Okay. We need to find somewhere to get you
                clothes – and somebody to give us some
                answers.

The Celestial Toymakers

A proposal for Big Finish's Villains Trilogy for the Fortieth Anniversary of DOCTOR WHO in 1993.

Rural English Village, 1930s...

A village that's got a hint of Royston Vasey about it, only in Cornwall or Devon. It's the sort of village you might find in horror movies, full of the 'Ooo-aaarrr-ing' yokels, who infest Transylvania in British horror movies. You know the sort. Always saying things like. "Ooooh, you don't want to up to that thur house on the hill thur, young maaaarster." Okay, maybe they're not THAT extreme, but it's the horror stereotype. And there is a haunted house – Windlesham Hall. In true horror style, the place has a history that would make Baskerville Hall look like a Wendy house. A history of dark and depraved goings on. There have been black masses, utterly foul lords of the manor, ghostly sightings, unexplained deaths, the full horror flick monty. The audio equivalent of a Hammer set-up. A young chap arrives and is told by the buxom serving wench (hey, we can't see that she's buxom but if this was a Hammer movie she would be, okay?) not to go to the house. Only bad can happen there. There's an evil in that house. Our young chap, Roger Windlesham, is the new Lord of the gaff and he's going to have a look at his country seat. He cajoles and persuades the comely serving lass (who we'd better give a name – how does Betty sound?) to show him the way out to his estate, where the servants will be waiting to meet him. She knows it's a bad idea, but she agrees. He's a smooth-tongued charmer, is Roger. You know what they say, Roger by name...

The Tardis is not happy. It's being hammered and battered about in the vortex. The vortex itself is all to hell. The patterns and rules of the vortex aren't being followed and the Tardis' controls are making even less sense than usual. The Doctor executes an emergency landing and arrives at Windlesham Hall a few moments before Roger and Betty. Newspapers have been delivered – the Times and the Devon Clarion (hopefully there's no such august publication). It's November 1930. The Doctor is up for investigating. When Roger arrives, he's a surprised to have guests, but he's pleased to have someone from London. He was worried that the locals were going to be a terrible bore (No offence, Betty). Roger has a bit of a low threshold for boredom. Still, he's been informed that there are ghosts, ghoulies and spooks around, which should keep things rather jolly. The Doctor's not keen on that, but he does want to know what's going on so he accepts Roger's offer of a meal and beds for the night. Inside, we meet the staff – again, they're stereotypes. Upright butler who's probably got a sinister secret, a dodgy housekeeper who's in on the secret as well. Peri begins to wonder at the stereotypes they're facing: 'It's like "Hound of the Baskervilles" crossed with "The Cat And The Canary". What? Hey, I like black and white movies, okay? I just don't want to be in one.' Getting ready for the dinner, Peri and Erimem find that their clothes have moved around the room. They didn't see it happen, but it did. Maybe it was a housekeeper or the maid. Except nobody else has been in the room. Weird.

Betty, meanwhile, has been invited to stay as well. She's eyeing young Roger as her way out of being a busty barmaid and into being the busty lady of the big house. (Again, playing up to stereotypes – not blatantly obvious but certainly floating around that area of comfortable recognition for the audience. They need to know the scenario.) Anyhoo, she's on her way down to dinner, probably after warning Peri and Erimem to keep their claws out of Roger – she saw him first and she's got dibs on him. And then she sees someone – something? – in the shadows. She takes a look. Talks to this figure – doesn't get an answer and when she gets closer she gets worried. She asks the usual questions a doomed stooge asks in horror movies. "Who are you? What are you doing in there? What...?" Followed by a blood-curdling SCREAM! When Betty is found, she's wearing a huge grin. She's deader than Cliff Richard's underpants but she's got a huge, off-putting, creepy grin on her face. Everybody has an alibi. Could it be the ghost of Roger's rotten ancestor? The one who had a branch of the Hellfire Club? Ever since he was killed by an uprising of his farm-workers over the matter of a farm-girl's virtue, his spirit has been rumoured to have stalked the hall, taking his vengeance on women, men and anybody else. The Doctor doesn't believe in ghosts here but there is something wrong. It's as if he knows the set-up just too well. (By now, the comfy territory we're in should start to get a bit uncomfortable.)

From here, we stay in familiar haunted house/Agatha Christie territory for the rest of part one, although it does get a bit weird, just how well the set-up is known to Peri and the Doctor. Lots of red herrings, clues, chills until the Doctor puts together the pieces. He works out what's going on. Or at least 99% of it. The villain is...

Wait! Roger doesn't want the Doctor to name the villain. **He** has to do it. The Doctor shakes off Roger's protests and names the villain (whoever it is and whoever the clues and red haddocks... sorry, herrings led him to). Roger goes mental as the Doctor reveals the villain (who isn't too put out by it all). But Roger really goes bing-bong do-lally. It's not right. It's not fair. He would have got it. He could have got it. The Doctor goes to pains to point out that this isn't right at all – they're in some kind of charade. Some kind of elaborate hoax. Why doesn't the perpetrator show himself? Roger is still protesting that he would have got it.

"But you didn't," replies a rich voice. It comes from everywhere in the Hall, but from nowhere it particular. The Hall fades away and is replaced by another locale – say, a London street, the surface of an asteroid. It doesn't really matter. The Hall is gone, so are all the people who were in it – Peri, Erimem and Roger included. There's only the Doctor and the Toymaker, who introduces himself again and congratulates the Doctor on solving his little puzzle. End of part one.

That only really works if the Toymaker's presence was being kept under wraps. If he was plonked on the front cover, his appearance at the end of ep 1 would be a bit of a non-shocker. Kind of like the Daleks turning up at the end of episode 1 of every story called "The Something of the Daleks".

Anyway, the Toymaker would send the Doctor into another scenario. It's not just games here – it's more along the lines of mysteries and puzzles. Not just Agatha Christie stuff. Different places and problems, though the same characters turn up in different personas wherever they go. The Doctor gets one set, Peri and Erimem another. Roger is involved as well. He seems to be another of the Toymaker's playthings, railing against the Toymaker, but we only find out the truth about him when he actually wins a game/challenge against the Toymaker. The

Toymaker is scared of him. Y'see, Roger is also the Toymaker.

As I remember them, past stories with the Toymaker have always taken place on his turf, so to speak. He's always been the mover and shaker, setting the scene for the story.

How about if he's on the defensive for a change?

The Toymaker has created a duplicate of himself. Another Toymaker – a different body and a different voice – a separate entity, a different person, a life in its own right. Ideal for the Toymaker, you'd think. Someone to challenge him through eternity, someone to push him to the limit, someone to keep him intrigued. Just one problem – the 2nd Toymaker (who's a bit Eddie Izzard-ish in my noggin) is too precise a replica. He's got a heightened sense of the twisted, the nasty and the sneaky. He's beating the Toymaker and if things don't turn about quickly, the original Toymaker will be a goner. (Whenever the two Toymakers are together, they'll play word games, trying to catch each other out, always trying to one-up the other, always trying to be get as victory). The original Toymaker needs help and turns to the only person he thinks can help him – the only person to have ever beaten him – the Doctor.

So the Doctor is stuck in the middle between two Toymakers, each of whom wants to destroy the other, and wants the Doctor's help to do it. Naturally, the Doctor's not daft enough to believe either of them, or the vast promises they make him, but he can't stay about in this place forever either. He's being pressured into choosing by the Toymakers putting Peri and Erimem into steadily more inescapable problems. The women are staying alive by living on their wits. They're smart, intelligent and resourceful, but they can't keep going forever.

A final challenge is decided upon. The two Toymakers in a last battle to see who survives. That's fine by the Doctor. While they're busy doing that, he'll see about finding a way of escape for himself and his friends. But that's just not happening. The Toymakers have chosen their game – and they've chosen their players. One will have Peri play for them, the other will have Erimem and it's a game to the death. For the game to end, either Peri or Erimem has to die. Of course, neither woman will kill the other. They're friends, they're close. They won't do it. The Toymakers have to agree. So they wipe the minds of both Peri and Erimem. It's as if they never met and don't know each other. One must kill the other.

The game is played out. Let's play up the idea that Erimem's going to die. We know Peri's fate – well, at least three alternative versions of it. (And the telly bottled out of the only one I liked – so now I reckon that Doctor nipped back later, picked up Peri, they had a couple more adventures then she lived happily ever after nowhere near Yrcanos or wrestlers. But I digress). But we don't know what happens to Erimem. Well, you might, but we don't. Maybe she will die here. It comes down to the end of the game – maybe it's a hunt of some kind – certainly nastier than the games in the sixties serial – and one has to kill the other to survive. But neither will do it. Peri won't kill. Neither will Erimem, even though she did kind of kill people in the battle at Giza. She's changing as a person and something inside tells her that killing this woman wouldn't be right. And so now they start to wonder about why they're trying to kill each other. Who set them to do this? They take the only alternative they have – they sit down and refuse to fight.

Stalemate. Both Toymakers go ballistic. They can't have a result if Peri and Erimem won't play. They want to start again but the Doctor points out that it won't make any difference. Taking away their memories didn't change who Peri and Erimem were. They're the same people they always were and if they're put into another game, they'd do the same. They won't play or fight for the Toymakers anymore. The Doctor pushes the Toymakers into expending huge amounts of their energies. He goads them, cajoles them, bullies them, manipulates them, until they are at each others' throats. They are tearing their universe apart to destroy each other. The Doctor grabs Peri and Erimem and they escape. A decidedly rough journey but they make it through. Peri and Erimem are closer friends because of what they went through. There's a huge blast of energy and the Toymaker's realm disappears. Is he destroyed? Did the Toymakers wipe each other out? No idea, answers the Doctor. He fancies a cup of tea.

Inside the Toymaker's domain, the battle is ending. The Toymaker, the original, is winning. He has his replica – Roger

– beaten down and worn out. Roger expects to be destroyed but the Toymaker holds back. He'll give Roger a chance. A game of chance...

Notes

Late in 2002 I got an email from Gary Russell inviting me to be one of a bunch of people pitching their ideas for a Celestial Toymaker story for the Fortieth anniversary. I knew I wasn't the only writer invited to pitch for that story. Gary was upfront about that. One thing I always liked about working with Gary was how open and honest he was. He is a brilliant director and script editor to work with. I learned a huge amount from him about writing for audio and radio. I will always be enormously grateful to him.

The brief was the Fifth Doctor against the Celestial Toymaker. I *think* Peri and Erimem were mentioned as the companions but writing this fourteen years on, I can't be certain of that.

So… what can you do with the Celestial Toymaker in a sequel? I reread the rather disappointing Target novelisation of the story and then reread The Nightmare Fair. I started thinking about the Toymaker and why the Fifth Doctor would have wound up in conflict with him. They could have met by chance again or the Toymaker could have come looking for revenge but those seemed very dull and mundane reasons for an adventure to take place. So I turned the idea of revenge on its head. What if the Toymaker *needed* the Doctor? That interested me. Now *why* would the Toymaker need the Doctor? He would have to be in trouble, surely? Okay, so the Toymaker is in trouble, now how did that happen? He exists to play his challenges and games. The Doctor is the only one who has ever beaten him… what if he's on the verge not only being beaten again, but of actually being killed? That made me wonder what kind of enemy could the Toymaker face who could seriously have the chance to kill him? And what kind of enemy would induce the Doctor to help such a powerful enemy? I found the answer when I asked who the Toymaker would look to face as an enemy… if he wanted to face someone who could challenge him constantly, surely the person he should face was himself?

So it was the Toymaker versus the Toymaker?

That interested me. The Toymaker created a second

Toymaker… and the second Toymaker was winning. He was nastier than the original Toymaker, more vicious and more evil. For the Doctor, saving his old enemy would be saving the lesser of two extreme evils.

So I had my basic hook for the story – two Toymakers.

What kind of games would they play?

The first thing was that it had to be different from the 1966 TV story. It couldn't just be the Toymakers sitting playing chess. The idea of a game had to be expanded into something broader. I starting thinking about the murder weekends and the movie *Clue*, which was based on the board game Cluedo. If I set it in a country house and played the first episode as an Agatha Christie style whodunit, I could pull the audience towards the belief that we were in Christie territory with the story and then use one of the cliffhangers to completely undermine their expectations and hit them with the Toymaker.

As soon as I had all of that in place, I only needed to work out a personality for the Second Toymaker. I initially thought of him as a charming Kenneth Brannagh type of fellow, but then I started to look at later in the piece when he became more manic and hysterical. I had no doubt a smoothie like Kenneth Brannagh could do that but he quickly morphed into Eddie Izzard in my head. I am a huge fan of Eddie Izzard, though not of all of his films. However, in my head he was the basis for this ne Toymaker, and suddenly I could really feel the dynamic between the two Toymakers. An older tired Michael Gough and a manic young Eddie Izzard, battling each other with the Doctor and his companions in the middle trying to save the universe.

We heard pretty quickly that the Toymaker story wasn't going ahead. Later on I heard that Michael Gough didn't want to do it. He was pretty much retired by then. The rumour I heard was that my proposal hadn't been selected anyway. What I heard was the Craig Hinton's story had been chosen. I don't know if that is true or not but if it is, I can't complain. I only knew Craig through discussions and chats online but I hugely enjoyed those chats. He was a lovely, delightful man, who is greatly missed by his friends. He claimed to have created the word *fanwank*, which should be enough to make anyone like him. If I was going to lose out to him, I won't complain about that.

Looking at the proposal I did wonder if there was anything I could have done to make it better. The first thing would be to pull the Doctor to the fore a lot more. He is largely a passenger in the story, observing what is happening in episode one and also observing in later episodes how the Toymakers are using and manipulating Peri and Erimem. The companions have a lot more to do than the Doctor and that's not how it should be. The show is *Doctor Who* not *Companion Who*. I think I would have added sidekicks for the Toymakers so that they could scheme against each other and the Doctor would deal with those schemes, acting as a referee. That would give him a number of different plots to take part in simultaneously and keep to the fore.

I would also have played up the danger to the universe of the younger, less stable Toymaker being victorious. I'd have shown how he would have been a threat to all of time and space, possibly by having them play out one of their games on Earth and causing huge amounts of death and damage. That would really give the Doctor a reason to stop him, otherwise there would be a real temptation to think the Toymakers deserve each other and have the Doctor escape and let them have at each other.

The title *The Celestial Toymakers* was a working title. That could never have been the title if it had been produced. It gives away a huge plot point. Titles are really important, even at the early stage of a story's evolution. I now edit a range of books featuring the Fifth Doctor's companion, *Erimem*. One of the novels, *A Pharaoh of Mars*, which was written by Jim Mortimore came from him seeing the title *A Pharaoh of Mars* in one of the guideline documents. I had a short story in mind for that title but it sparked a completely different story in Jim's head, so I gave him the title and came up with a different title for my short. Always try to give your story a good title, even at early stages. It's really worthwhile. Sometimes I use a working title just for myself, because it focuses my mind on what the story is about.

.

UNBOUND
COLD COMFORT

An audio play proposed as a potential continuation of Big Finish's DOCTOR WHO UNBOUND series of stories.

"A cosmos without the Doctor scarcely bears thinking about..."

What if the Doctor didn't always save the day?
What if the Doctor didn't get the bat's milk on Androzani Minor?
What if the Doctor died?

What is the Doctor? We know he's a Time Lord but what *is* he? Really? "A moral force charging through the galaxy" is roughly what RTD called him in Confidential. He's the universe's protector, the champion of the weak and oppressed, a beacon of hope, something to believe in, someone we can trust to be there when things seem hopeless. But what if he wasn't there anymore? What if he finally lost? What if he died? What would the universe do without the Doctor? And what would his legacy be? What lasting effect would he have had? On the universe and on his friends.

On Androzani Minor, the 5th Doctor carries Peri into the Tardis. He didn't get the bat's milk for Peri. She's going to die. The Doctor is in despair. He has failed his friend and now he knows they'll both die. It's a riff on the scene from The Caves of Androzani but changed slightly, to be more despairing, without the visits from the past and without the change into Colin Baker. The Doctor tells himself that he's going to die and then slumps without the regeneration we know and expect. The Tardis takes off, the long, full take-off to show something is happening - and then the sound fades and there's the hum of the Tardis... and then that fades too as if the Tardis is dying along with the Doctor.

Aiko Chen is half Japanese, half Korean, all London - and she's a nurse at a cottage hospital in Kent in 2005. She's cycling to work, late at night in a thunderstorm, muttering and grumbling about choosing this place to work when she sees a blue box immediately in front of her, as if it had appeared in a flash of lightning. She almost crashes into it and falls off her bike as she avoids the box. She's just getting to her feet when the box opens and a woman topples out, burbling incoherent nonsense. The door swings shut behind her. Aiko uses her mobile to call for an ambulance. The woman rambles on and it becomes clear that it's Peri - but she seems to be insane.

In hospital, Peri is sedated and blood tests are taken. The police and doctors ask Aiko questions (well, a doctor does but it's implied a non-speaking copper is nearby) but she has no answers about this mystery woman.

At this point, meteorologists are becoming worried by the changing weather around Earth. Drought is becoming more widespread, the poles are melting quicker, causing critical desalination of the Atlantic threatening an ice age, wild storms are hitting Australia, America and Europe- and a ream of other threats that have been talked about for years except that they're all happening at once and they're all getting much, much worse very quickly. And as usual, in Britain it's raining.

The Fifth Doctor is apologising to Peri. He's sorry. He didn't mean for this to happen. It's his fault and he's sorry. Peri wakes and is disoriented. She has been dreaming. She has to find this man. That's the top priority on her mind. Find the man in her dreams. Except she has no idea where he is - or even who he is. Aiko looks in, expecting to see Peri still out for the count and is surprised to find her up and about. She settles Peri and discovers that Peri doesn't even know her own name - she has no memory at all. Aiko tells Peri the story of how they met and Peri slumps back into her bed, apparently asleep. When Aiko is out of the way, Peri sneaks out of her room, snags a uniform and sneaks out of the hospital (very much a nod to Spearhead From Space but without the shower scene) and she makes her way to the Tardis. She vaguely recognises it but doesn't know what it is. It's a memory that's just out of reach. She collapses by the Tardis and is found by Aiko whose first reaction is to get Peri to a psych ward but something stops her - she agrees to help Peri back into the hospital. If nobody missed her, Aiko won't spill the beans.

A weather satellite that's being redirected to observe the hurricane that just hit the Cayman Islands catches sight of something. The German scientist watching on screen can't decipher what it is - and then the picture frazzes out - the satellite is gone.

There has been a problem with Peri's blood tests. She is

something very wrong with her blood.

Peri has another nightmare. She is talking with the Doctor. Again he is apologising, blaming himself for what has happened, blaming himself for not being there to deal with what's coming. At the end of the dream Peri is asking why he's sorry and what's coming. "What's coming? What's coming, Doctor?" She wakes abruptly, aware that the man she saw in her dream was the Doctor. She doesn't know more than that but she knows that he was the Doctor and that he called her Peri. Aiko heads off to check that with the records.

The pictures taken from the satellite are examined and they cause a huge stir when Sky News broadcasts them - a spaceship is seen in the last few frames and is also seen to take out the satellite. Earth's weather problems are being caused by the spaceship. There is panic around the world. Governments call for calm - and occasionally accuse each other of owning the spaceship, calling it a strategic weapons platform.

Watching the pictures on TV, Peri is fascinated. She recognises the ship. She's saying as much when her psychiatric specialist arrives and turns the TV off. He has some test results. Her blood is severely messed up and she'll have to go for more tests. He thinks she's a junkie. Without thinking, Peri says it's probably the Spectrox. And then she wonders where that came from. She has no idea what Spectrox is. Neither does the specialist but it boosts his theory that she's a druggie - especially after he reads the results of Aiko's checking on her. Peri Brown, disappeared from Lanzarotte in 1983 and her family haven't heard from her since - that's 22 years ago. He leaves Peri alone. She collapses back onto her bed - and tries to force herself to remember. Peri Brown... American... Lanzarotte... a fair-haired Doctor... was she ill in Lanzarotte? When the nurses and doctors are distracted by the TV news about the sighting of a spaceship, Peri sneaks off and uses the computer terminal, calling up her medical file both here and in America. A vague mention of the odd content of her blood and the word 'Spectrox' being suggested as a new drug on the market. She then hacks into the police file on her disappearance. She finds that the fair-haired man wasn't *a* doctor but known as The Doctor. She does some searching and is caught by Aiko who tries to shoo her off back to bed - but Peri is blithely hacking into secure government and UN files. She discovers the Doctor's involvement with defence agencies. A scientific adviser and a bit of a VIP. And then Aiko's chatter fades and the Doctor is talking to Peri. He tells her that she can remember, she knows she can. She mustn't force it but she'll remember. She wonders if she's going mad hearing the voice of someone who isn't there, talking to him without Aiko being aware of it. He tells her that she isn't mad but she's been through an ordeal. She should think of him as nothing more than a minor irritation. Her subconscious giving her a nudge in the right direction. Peri grumbles that he's hardly Jiminy Crickett. And cricket rings a bell with her. Cricket. Something about the Doctor and cricket... Aiko's bemused. There's a spaceship in orbit and her mystery patient has just hacked into restricted government files. Fading away the Doctor tells Peri that she'll find the truth in the Tardis. And while Peri doesn't remember exactly what the Tardis is, she knows it has something to do with the police box. And now she knows that the Doctor is her friend.

Aiko is coming off duty and finds Peri changing into her clothes - shorts and a tied blouse - not the thing for this weather and not for a woman in her mid 30s either. She gives Peri a lab coat to wear over her clothes - it might keep some of the rain off. Aiko's not worried about getting into trouble for helping a patient go for a walk - the aliens are a much bigger threat. They've been hailed and are refusing to respond. The governments are taking that as them being hostile.

At the Tardis, Peri recognises it as being the Doctor's, as being safe, as being home. They get the spare key from the cubby-hole above the P on the police box and go inside. Aiko expects it to be cramped. Instead it's large and pitch black. She trips over something on the floor and fishes out her mobile phone. The phone has a small light on it and gives an idea of the real scale of the room. It's not possible. When Peri speaks for the first time inside the Tardis, the console room begins to slowly come back to life. The lights rise slowly and the hum begins to rise in recognition. Aiko's agog at what she sees around her - the scale of the console room, but Peri's more interested in what she sees on the ground. The Doctor's clothes are abandoned. Does that means he's somewhere else inside the Ship? Why did she call it a ship? And then memories come flooding back to her. Snatches of conversations with the Doctor, recognisable words and sentences from their time and adventures together... Turlough, Trion, Erimem, Queen Anne, Kamelion, diamond, Jubal Eustace, Constantine, Tibet, Androzani... words fly at her in a jumble in her voice and in the Doctor's, washing over her and forcing the memories back to the front of her mind. She screams as she remembers everything - everything up to her death from Spectrox Toxaemia. What she doesn't know is what happened after that. Why is she now 15 years older than she was and where is the Doctor? What happened in those intervening, lost 15 years? She heads into the Tardis, looking for the Doctor, but apart from the console room, everything is dead, waiting. The Doctor's not there, and he's not the sort to turn nudist. Peri wonders if she could have taken 15 years to recover from the poisoning... the Tardis could have helped her survive... (would it be more potent to have the Doctor's body in the console room rather than just his clothes?). Whether the Doctor's body is there or not, Peri knows he's dead - a real moment of emotion for a lost friend. A bleak, bleak moment as the Doctor's death affects Peri. Aiko notes that the world could probably really use the Dcotor about now. Peri turns on the scanner for the latest on the alien ship. It's landing - in Antarctica. Just past the (fictional) Scott Ice Shelf, a huge chunk of snow and ice that hangs over a bay on the Southern continent. Helicopters and fighter planes have been dispatched to meet the visitors and similarities are drawn to a previous landing at a Southern polar base. There's hope that these visitors will be friendlier. Peri doesn't think so - "A warm welcome isn't in their nature.". And then the helicopters and planes are shot down, blasted from the skies. An Ice Warrior speaks - the Southern continent now belongs to them. Anyone approaching will be destroyed. And there's no Doctor to stop them. (This would be the place for a cliff-hanger.)

Peri doesn't think the Ice Warriors are likely to settle for part of a planet. The Tardis' instruments tell her that the Ice

Warriors have been influencing the Earth's weather patterns. So they're up to something. What are the options? Let the politicians and army deal with it? Not an options, really. The politicians would argue and the soldiers would get killed. The Tardis already shows Ice Warriors at work at the edge of the Scott Ice Shelf. It looks as if they're building a perimeter. Peri isn't so sure. Something's not right about the placing of their encampments. And as she speaks, her light American accent occasionally slips into a more mature, English one. When she's picked up on it, she thinks it must be something that happened in fifteen forgotten years with the Doctor. Peri is tempted to hand the Tardis over to the military but she shudders to think what the military - and worse, the politicians - would do with this technology. What would the Doctor do? He'd march in and ask them to stop the invasion and to clear out. Aiko's not impressed by this as a plan. "Too bad," says Peri. "Because if it's good enough for the Doctor it's good enough for me." She doesn't sound at all convinced that she'll succeed. She's almost reluctant to go but feels she has to and blames the Doctor for her stupidity in doing this. Aiko has the chance to leave but doesn't - she doesn't fully understand that the Tardis is a vehicle. Peri closes the doors and sets the Tardis in motion. Somewhere in her past she's learned how to pilot the Tardis. They head off to the wardrobe in search of warm clothing.

A team of British soldiers are on manoeuvres in Antarctica - these are black ops. On a scrambled channel they get the word to go. They are to take out the Ice Warriors but keep the ship intact if at all possible.

Peri and Aiko are dressed for the polar conditions - thick, thermal outer clothes and warmer clothes underneath for Aiko. Peri has gone for something more distinctive under the thermal parka and trousers. They'll be landing soon at one of the line of outposts the Ice Warriors have built along their perimeter. They should be military outposts but the guns seem to be pointing downwards - and she doesn't think it's the Ice Warriors being friendly.

The Ice Warriors are preparing to do something - something big. They're enjoying the cold but they're busy preparing for whatever they're planning. And whatever it is, it's going to give the planet to them.

The Tardis materialises, masked by a chunk of ice lifted through the glacier and its noise carried away by the fierce winds blowing in a blizzard. Having had some time to think more clearly, Peri's amended her plan - she'll see what the Ice Warriors are up to and then get the information back to the authorities. Aiko likes this better. She's gobsmacked when they step out into the Antarctic though. And impressed. The Tardis could save her a fortune on foreign holidays... They set off, planning a to have a sneaky look at the Ice Warriors' operations.

Also sneaking in under cover of the blizzard is the British army outfit, commanded by Captain Gallagher. He's just issuing final orders for a precise strike against the enemy when his NCO spots Peri and Aiko entering the projected battle zone.

Peri and Aiko spot an Ice Warrior on patrol and take cover. Aiko is again gobsmacked - her first sighting of a genuine alien. "It's not a little green man - it's a sodding huge green man." She's amazed by how calmly Peri takes to seeing aliens - as if it was an everyday occurrence. Which it is. They make it to the Ice Warrior equipment. Sure enough it's a gun emplacement, capable of 360 degree rotation and firing from ground to sky, but it seems to be guarding something else - something akin to a drill. Why would they be drilling here at the pole? Why come to Earth to drill at all? They don't need oil... They are about to sneak out when an Ice Warrior spots them. They make a run for it and manage to hit the Ice Warrior with a swinging piece of equipment on its gun - but it marches straight through. Peri demands to speak to the Ice Lord which confuses the Ice Warrior for a moment. How does she know about the Ice Lords? And then there's gunfire and the soldiers emerge from the snow, gunning down the Ice Warrior. It takes a lot of bullets to put him down and they eventually have to use explosives. The second and third Ice Warriors at the site are despatched with grenades and armour piercing rounds. Peri is relieved and then irate at the way the Martians were killed. There was no need for them all to be killed. Aiko is grateful anyway. Gallagher wonder what they were doing, and Peri fills in the blanks - as many as suit her anyway. Seeing what they could find out about the Ice Warriors before reporting it back to the authorities. She doesn't mention the Tardis and from her manner, Gallagher assumes she's a scientist.

PERI: What makes you think that?

GALLAGHER: Who else is down here apart from penguins and scientists?

PERI: And soldiers?

GALLAGHER: On manoeuvres. So you are scientists?

PERI: Aiko's a nurse. I should be a botanist.

GALLAGHER: Instead of playing Jane Bond out here? But you're the only scientific brain we have so it looks like you're it. What are they up to here?

PERI: I'm not sure, but it looks like they're drilling into the ice using a sonic drill - their weapons are all sonic, by the way.

GALLAGHER: Sound?

PERI: Not ordinary sound. If they hit you with a blast it'll be like your insides are being microwaved and whisked at the same time. The question is, why are they drilling here? And why have they been affecting Earth's weather?

GALLAGHER: Good questions. Got any good answers to go with them?

PERI: Not yet. I'm kind of new to this job.

GALLAGHER: This drill. Can we use it as a weapon?

PERI: We can use it as a bargaining tool. If the Ice Warriors know we can hurt them there doesn't need to be any more bloodshed.

GALLAGHER: We've got their drill and some of their weapons. That should put us in a strong bargaining position. Right. I'll give you a radio and when you're out of range you can send an encoded signal. We have a nuclear sub off-coast waiting.

DOCTOR: Don't trust him.

PERI: What?

GALLAGHER: I said we have a sub off coast.

DOCTOR: Don't trust him.

PERI: What do you mean?

GALLAGHER: I mean me and my men are taking it from here.

DOCTOR: Do you trust him, Peri? Really trust him? Trust your instincts to make the right decision.

PERI: Doctor?

GALLAGHER: What are you talking about?

PERI: The Doctor - a doctor. Do you have one?

GALLAGHER: No.

PERI: Then we should stay with you. My friend's a nurse and I bet I know more first aid than any of you. Look, this is international territory and you can't order us to do anything.

GALLAGHER: I could shoot you for getting in the way.

PERI: Then you kill the only scientific mind here and the only medical professional. But it's up to you.

GALLAGHER: Bloody women. If you fall behind, we leave you, right?

PERI: Deal.

GALLAGHER: (moving off)
Right, you lot. Get this gear dismantled and ready to move.

AIKO: (quietly)
Peri, what's going on? Why the change in plan?

PERI: I'm not sure... I just thought the Doctor would have kept an eye on them.

AIKO: The Doctor's dead, Peri.

PERI: I know - but he means something. Him and everything he did. He has to. Or all the good he did was for nothing.

AIKO: You can't take his place.

PERI: I can try. I have to try. You can stay here if you like. You'll be safe in the Tardis.

AIKO: On my own? In that thing? Not on your nellie. You're still a patient. And the way you go about things I'll bet money you'll need a nurse before long.

PERI: Optimist, aren't you? But thanks - for coming.

AIKO: Where else would I go? Seriously. We're in the middle of nowhere and I can't drive that box of yours.

PERI: Thanks anyway. I...
(yells in pain)

AIKO: I've got you. What is it?

PERI: I don't know. It's passing now. Dizziness and a stabbing pain in the head.

AIKO: I'm not surprised. You should still be in hospital. It's probably that Spectrox stuff you were talking about.

PERI: I'm perfectly fine now. Fit as a flea.

Except Peri doesn't believe that. She wonders if she's going insane - is that a side effect of the Spectrox too? They head for the Ice Warriors' ship. Peri suggests a route for them to use for approach, which would hide them and give them space to set up the Martian guns before making contact. The question is, how do they make contact without being blasted to oblivion as soon as the Ice Warriors see them?

PERI: The Doctor might just walk up and knock.

Which she does, heading off before anyone can object, muttering to herself that Doctor always made this kind of thing look nonchalant and easy. She skirts the ridges of ice they're using for shelter and uses cover and the blizzard to get to the spaceship. To her surprise she's caught up by Gallagher, though it becomes clear he's there to stop her rather than talk.

They're spotted by the Ice warriors and taken inside the ship for questioning.

Aiko is concerned for Peri. Her new chum has been under a lot of pressure and is acting very oddly. Though odd would seem to be situation normal for Peri.

Peri and Gallagher are marched to meet the Ice Lord. They're in deep trouble when the Ice Lord finds that Gallagher was carrying an Ice Warrior's gun. He finds out that one of the outposts isn't reporting in. Posturing between the Ice Lord and Gallagher - threatening each other with, at various points, death, genocide and destruction of the spaceship. Peri seems aloof and above it all. She waits until there's a lull and starts talking. The American in her accent is almost gone now and she seems rooted with the slightly more mature, English voice. She remains flippant but more focused.

PERI: Captain Gallagher's telling the truth. His
                    men have one of your own battle-turrets
                    aimed at the ship as well as a mining
                    lance. That should be more than enough
                    to turn this ship of yours into… well, an
                    even bigger pile of scrap metal than it
                    already is. Is this the best ship you could
                    manage? No wonder you're looking to
                    settle down. You must be scared the
                    sellotape and string holding this thing
                    together will fall apart. Sending one of
                    your men out? Tell him to shut the door
                    after him. Don't want you catching cold,
                    do we? Hang on, what's this?

GALLAGHER: Looks like a map.

PERI: Well, you're not bright but your
                    eyesight's good. It was a rhetorical
                    question. But it is a map. And it shows
                    where our Martian chums here have their
                    drill-sites. Here, here, here… all along the
                    edge of the land-mass under the ice-

shelf…
(pause then angry)
…you maniacs.

GALLAGHER: What is it?

PERI: Can't you see what they're planning to
do? Those laser drill of theirs are going to
shear off the ice shelf.

GALLAGHER: And?

PERI: It's the size of a country, man! The force
when it plunges into the ocean will send a
tidal wave like this planet hasn't seen
since before man was here. The force of it
will take islands off the map, islands as
far north as Britain and America will
disappear, hundreds of millions - billions
will die.

ICE LORD: And as humanity reels we will melt the
ice, taking the salt content of the water to
such a low level that the climate will
change. The poles will stretch out.

PERI: The poles will cover the bulk of the
planet. The rest will be desert.

ICE LORD: And a few temperate zones to grow food
for all of our people.

GALLAGHER: All of you? How many of you are there?
A ship this size can't have more than a
few dozen. A bit light to colonise a whole
planet.

PERI: Oh, there are more of them. Tens of
thousands of them, scattered across the

	galaxy. Most of them are honourable people but a few cling to their old ways. Conquest, conflict… the same boring rubbish they were so bad at before they lost their planet. Don't you ever learn?
GALLAGHER:	Should you be antagonising him this way?
PERI:	Probably not but I'm doing it anyway. It's what the Doctor would do. So, that's the sum of your plan, eh?
ICE LORD:	This will be a good home for us. A good place for our hatchlings.
PERI:	No. Sorry. The planet Earth would like to apologise to all green-skinned, scaly despots but it's currently occupied dealing with its own lunatics and doesn't have room for importing any new ones. Please try again in around a thousand years.
GALLAGHER:	Are you trying to get us killed?
PERI:	No, that's your job - marching in here carrying one of their own guns. So, Ice Lord, given that you have weapons aimed at you, here's the deal. You leave Earth and go and find somewhere else to colonise, and nobody gets hurt.
GALLAGHER:	That's not the offer. She doesn't speak for the Earth. You and your people are my prisoners. You will be treated well and stand trial for you actions.
PERI:	Ignore him, he's an idiot.

ICE LORD: Silence. We must make our plans. You
                   will be interrogated soon. Svar, place
                   them in a cell.

Aiko's worried by Peri's behaviour. She tells the NCO as much.

AIKO: She should be in hospital. She's lost 15
                   years of her life and her friend,
                   boyfriend... whatever... she's coming to
                   terms with him being dead.

The NCO replies that if there's no word from Gallagher in 15 minutes, they have to attack the ship.

Peri and Gallagher are locked up. Peri is depressed by her failure to achieve anything. *Why did she bother? Did she really think she could emulate the Doctor and achieve something here? Why did she think she could? Too much time with the Doctor. But he wouldn't give up. He'd keep fighting. And look where it got him - dead. But she has to keep trying.* She starts mulling the Ice Warrior plan. Gallagher, on the other hand, is looking to do something practical. Something like escape or contact the sub waiting for them. The doors are solid but Peri manages to prise free a wall-panel. There's a relay which they can use to patch in the intercom to a transmitter - something she's learned from the Doctor, obviously. Gallagher sends a message to the sub, saying what the Ice Warriors are about to do to the ice shelf. Peri begins to wonder, running through the plan she saw. It won't work. There aren't quite enough Ice Warrior drilling sites for it to work.

PERI: What will the governments do when they
                   hear what the Ice Warriors are planning?

GALLAGHER: Probably hit the ship with nukes. Bad
                   luck for us. But it goes with the job. My
                   job anyway.

PERI: It's worse than that. Tell them not to fire
                    the nuclear missiles.

GALLAGHER: Are you mad?

PERI: Don't you see? It's what the Ice warriors
                    want. It's why we've been put into a room
                    where we could hack into
                    communications

The Ice Lord is listening and orders the communication
halted. The message that's been sent will be all they need.

Peri is explaining when the link goes dead. The nuclear
detonations will be the final push to dislodge the ice shelf. The
Ice Warriors will detect incoming missiles and take off long
before the nukes arrive. They've just set up humanity to destroy
itself and hand the world to the Ice Warriors. Peri has a strange
reaction - almost a fit. She slumps unconscious. Gallagher tries
to contact the NCO to have him attack the spaceship without
success.

Outside, the NCO is preparing the troops for battle when
they are attacked by Ice Warriors. The NCO is badly injured
and there are only a few soldiers left alive. Aiko almost goes
for a gun - but the threat of being killed puts her off.

Peri is having a conversation with the 5th Doctor. They're
discussing the situation she finds herself in.

DOCTOR: Well, this is a bit of a pickle, isn't it?

PERI: You don't say?

DOCTOR: How do you plan to get yourself out of it?
                    I assume you do have a plan?

PERI: (sarcastic)
                    Oh, yeah, like you always went into
                    things with a plan.

DOCTOR:	What do you mean?
PERI:	I mean, how could you let yourself die? People need you. I need you. Millions of people are going to die. You could stop it happening.
DOCTOR:	But?
PERI:	But you're dead. You're not here and now they're going to die. So am I. And there's nothing I can do about it.
DOCTOR:	Not if you're going to sit there snivelling and feeling sorry for yourself.
PERI:	What did you say? You son of a bi...
DOCTOR:	Do you remember our time together?
PERI:	Of course. Well, now I do.
DOCTOR:	And what happened in the Tardis? At the end?
PERI:	No. Not after you carried me in.
DOCTOR:	Oh, dear. That *is* inconvenient.
PERI:	Inconvenient? I'm trapped on an Ice Warrior ship, the world's about to end and I'm hallucinating that I'm talking to a dead friend and you call my memory problems inconvenient?
DOCTOR:	Let's see if I can give your memories a bit of a nudge, shall we?

PERI:	Forget my memories. Just tell me how to…
DOCTOR:	Good luck.
	(beat)
	Contact.

The prisoners are loBbed in beside Gallagher and the unconscious Peri. Aiko is about to attend her when Peri wakes with a scream. She recovers quickly and seems aloof. She has a plan of sorts. It's not a great plan. In fact it's suicidally dangerous and probably stupid. She opens the wall panel again and begins to cross-join circuits and hot-wire the alien-looking technology.

GALLAGHER:	Can you get us contact with the sub again?
PERI:	Nope.
GALLAGHER:	Control of the ship?
PERI:	Nope.
GALLAGHER:	Door control?
PERI:	Nope.
GALLAGHER:	What then?

Sound of sparks and flames. Burning.

PERI:	(cheerfully, blithely)
	I'm setting fire to the ship.
GALLAGHER:	Are you completely mental?
PERI:	More than likely. We'll soon find out.

An alarm sounds. After a moment, the door opens automatically. They get out sharply and a few seconds later the door closes again. Peri knew how much the Ice Warriors hate heat and gambled that they'd give themselves a brief chance to escape. Gallagher points out how stupid that is - but Peri states that not everyone thinks the same way as humans. So now they're loose on the ship with the Ice Warriors coming for them. Escape isn't Peri's plan. They have to get control of the communications to stop the sub firing nuclear missiles. Too late. The announcement comes that Warriors should secure themselves. The humans' nuclear missiles are incoming. The ship will be taking off almost immediately, radio traffic is jammed so that the humans won't be able to order the missiles to self-destruct when the take-off is noticed. The ship has escape pods and Peri orders the others to the pods - she is becoming more assured, more commanding, more Doctor-like. She needs the humans off the ship so she can set the engines to over load and destroy the ship. She plans to give the Ice Warriors time to get to the escape pods as well and doesn't want the two sides clashing there. She heads for the engine room. Aiko and Gallagher follow, ignoring her protests. They manage to get the Ice Warriors who work the engine room under lock and key (or the equivalent) and Peri sets the engines to blow. The Ice Lord turns up to stop her, shooting Gallagher (an injury, not fatal). He is about to kill Aiko, so Peri has no option but to lower shields around the engine, unleashing waves of heat, incapacitating the Ice Lord. She raises the shields again but locks the engines to overload before scampering for the ships control bridge. The Ice Lord is weakly heard over the intercom telling Warriors to abandon ship. On the bridge, Peri is tracking the incoming nukes. The communication codes are encrypted and would take too long to break. They'll just have to shoot the missiles down. She sends Gallagher to handle the guns and deals with the piloting herself. She warns them that they'll have to get this right - there won't be a second chance. She throws the ship into a curve.

AIKO: Peri, where did you learn to do that?
                    Earlier you couldn't control your own

271

ship. Who are you? Really.

PERI: I know who I am, Aiko. I remember it all. Androzani Minor, the Spectrox, lying dying in the Tardis… dying… both of us dying. I know who I am. I'm Peri Brown - and I'm the Doctor.

Gallagher manages to shoot down the missiles (just in time) and they abandon ship just before it explodes.

Peri heads back to the Tardis while Gallagher gets his troops together. She's already planning to give the Ice Warriors a lift back to a planet where there are others of their people - but she'll have to do it so that they don't try to take over the Tardis. Aiko asks what she means about being the Doctor. She explains.

PERI: We were dying, both of us. If the Doctor had got the bat's milk we'd both have survived but he didn't. It wasn't his fault. He tried, I know that. So we were dying of Spectrox poisoning.

AIKO: Never heard of it. Apart from you.

PERI: You wouldn't have. It's not local.

AIKO: Alien? You were on another planet?

PERI: Naturally. The Doctor knew he was dying. I knew it was the end for me as well. Odd, I wasn't angry or bitter. I just sort of accepted it. The Doctor didn't, though. The anguish he felt at letting me die… I can feel his guilt, remember it… terrible. The Tardis knew we were both dying as well. Somehow, it found what little life was left in each of us and pulled it all together, merging us into one. It kick-started a regeneration - a rebirth if you like. It's something the Doctor's people - my people - do when they're dying. The Tardis couldn't save us individually but it could save us both, together. And here I am... I am the Doctor - with a bit of Peri thrown in for good measure. Pity it aged me though. Oh, I don't know. I haven't aged too badly. And the longer hair suits me. I may have grown an inch or two as well... When I regenerate next time I wonder if I'll stay a woman or change back? Could be embarrassing when it comes to clothes.

AIKO: You're barking mad.

PERI: If someone told you this morning that you'd have fought aliens in spaceships at the South Pole you wouldn't have believed that either. I can prove it all to you.

AIKO: How?

PERI: Come with me. There are alien planets, alien people, some friendly, some vicious, some with sixteen arms and no feet. If I show you the universe, will you believe me then?

AIKO: More likely I'll have myself sectioned.

PERI: Is that a yes? The universe isn't nearly as much fun when you travel alone. We could start by taking those Ice Warriors somewhere secure.

AIKO: Will it be safe?

PERI: Shouldn't think so for a moment.

AIKO: And you don't know what we'll meet
                   there?

PERI: Not really, no.

AIKO: I'd have to be mad to go with you.

PERI: Absolutely.

AIKO: Okay. I'm in.

Tardis door opens. Hum of the ship, content with the Doctor
back.

AIKO: This is insane, you know.

PERI: I know.

Doors close, Tardis take-off begins.

PERI: That's what makes it so much fun.

Perhaps an amended version of the theme tune - one
representing the nature of the Peri/Doctor fusion. Impulsive,
headstrong, kinetic...

The end, with Peri's transformation into the Doctor, is
supposed to a kind of vibe that would hint that everyone has the
ability to be just a bit like the Doctor and make a difference. It
wouldn't be bludgeoned out but it would be there as an
undertone. The story is very much a trad base-under-siege,
Earth-under-attack story. We thought it best to go for the most
traditional kind of Doctor Who story if we were going to see
how the world and Peri dealt with the invasion without the
Doctor. The Ice Warriors don't have to be Ice Warriors - they
can be a different race entirely, but we thought their familiarity
would be useful.

Notes

This was pitched to Big Finish a few years after the *Unbound* series of *Doctor Who* audio plays was released for the show's Fortieth anniversary. Claire and I proposed another. The *Unbound* series were based around the concept of 'what if…?'. There had been *'what if the Doctor had never left Gallifrey?'*, *'what if the Doctor hadn't been on Earth when UNIT needed him?'*, *'what if the Doctor thought the ends justified the means?'*… there had been six different Doctors, different angles on what we thought we knew of the Doctor and his universe. They were an interesting twist on the show.

So, what about this one, *Cold Comfort*?

Oh, dear. There's so much wrong with this as it stands. It feels more like a gimmick than a story. It might have been fun as part of the series marking the show's fortieth anniversary, but as a continuation of the series, I'm not sure it is special enough to merit actually being produced.

The first problem with the story is how incredibly obvious the central conceit is. The idea that the TARDIS would try to save both of its inhabitants by forcing them to merge is one I do like. So, the idea that Peri and the Doctor merge isn't bad. The way we handled it in the pitch was, and that was my fault rather than Claire's. I spent too much time with Peri dropping clues about what she might have become and didn't spend nearly enough time laying red herrings and putting down obfuscation to disguise what had happened. I should have played up more time at the beginning with Peri being the Peri we know, and then let the Doctor's consciousness start to seep through. At that point she could remember seeing him die. She could remember seeing his regeneration fail and she could remember that she'd had the only bat's milk, or that the TARDIS had somehow managed to save her. She could feel guilty about surviving and then when the Doctor starts talking to her she could have justified it as her mind coping with the guilt. Then at the hospital everything could have coalesced so that Peri started to understand what had happened. At the moment that is *sort of* what happens, but it's not clearly enough defined or well-enough structured. The line of evolution for the character from Peri to the Doctor needed to be much, much cleaner.

The character of the Peri Doctor needs more definition, too. The way it sits now, she's Peri and she's the Doctor and most of her character comes from our foreknowledge of those characters. I think she's lacking a moment where we say "yes, that's the Doctor". In The Christmas Invasion, David Tennant had the swordfight scene and that moment when he got rid of the villain with a tangerine. Matt Smith had his moment in The Eleventh Hour… "Basically, run…". I think we could have had a moment like that for Peri-Doctor if her character had been defined better within the story. We had discussed her personality. We saw her as a risk-taker, exuberant, funny, fiercely moral, a little bit cheeky and saucy and utterly fearless. I'm not sure that came through in the pitch.

Aiko didn't have a fully formed personality either. The idea was that she was brave, intelligent, bored and in search of something more interesting. We wanted her to reflect the Twenty-First Century, having parents of different nationalities, and having been raised in the wonderful cultural melting pot of London. If we'd had time to get to know Aiko, I think she would have been a lot of fun. However, she needed a lot more work in this intro story. We contemplated doing a full switch and giving a female Doctor a male companion, but we thought that two women rattling around the universe in the TARDIS would be much more fun.

I have a feeling that this might have been quite a disjoined story. The first half would have been set in England and the second half in Antarctica. Re-reading the pitch, those two halves do feel curiously unconnected. It reminds me of *Attack of the Cybermen*. The first half was set on Earth and the second half on Telos. I thought the first half of that story was a fascinating thing and the second half a disappointing, disjointed and unrelated mess. I don't think this story would have been as schismed as that one, but I do think it needed to be made to flow far better than it does in the pitch.

The soldiers needs work, too. I'm not unhappy with the Gallagher but like the Doctor and Aiko he needed a lot more work. He needed to be a living, breathing character rather than someone there to fulfil a purpose in the story. The conflict between him and Peri-Doctor seemed forced. I've no doubt that would all have been ironed out in drafting the script but if a pitch is going to sell there has to be more to the character than he has here.

The Ice Warriors were put in because I wanted something familiar in the story, to centre it on *Doctor Who*. The opening of episode one is a deliberate riff on the opening of *Spearhead From Space*, and we wanted something familiar. So, we went for the Ice Warriors. Making the plot about changing the environment kind of tied to Peri's interest in natural science. It's not exactly botany but it felt like it was in the same post code. In retrospect, the Ice Warriors seem rather superfluous and are thrown away by only being in half of the story. It would have been better to come up with something new so that when someone else used the Ice Warriors they'd have more impact.

If I'm honest, I think the whole thing feels like a first draft. I think Morecambe and Wise would describe it best. The ideas are all there, but not necessarily in the right order. There's an interesting and fun story in there but the pitch really needed work. The thing about writing a pitch is that you do get carried away with what you're writing. The bits you really like get the majority of your attention and you can occasionally miss some of the most important aspects of the story. It's always useful to let someone else have a read over your pitch. Get another writer to read it, to see what they think. There's a good chance that if there's something you've missed, they'll pick it up, especially if they're not immersed in the project you're working on. They'll bring a fresh eye and will ask questions that your producer or script editor is likely to ask. If they ask questions, take them seriously and address them. You can be too close to your own work. Now if Claire and I plot together, one of us writes and the other reads and asks questions. It's really worth getting a second pair of eyes on it.

It's also worth pointing out that this pitch is far too long and far too involved. Different producers and publishers want different size of pitches. I worked on a TV series which went through different levels of pitch. First there was a one paragraph pitch, which would be followed by a more detailed two page submission if the paragraph was liked. After that there would be a scene by scene breakdown of the story. The commission came if that was acceptable. Others have asked for a single A4 page or a maximum of two A4 pages. I'd say two A4 pages is a good length to aim at. You should be able to fit everything you need to say into two pages. You should be able to get plot, characterization and development into those two pages without rambling and getting carried away. These days I always aim at two pages as my rule of thumb. No more crazy-long pitches like this one.

All in all, I think *Cold Comfort* could have been interesting but it would have needed a hell of a lot of work on the pitch to get anyone interested.

KILL OR CURE

A proposal sent to BBV.

Katya Dylan (Kat to her pals and fans) is a presenter on a Blue Peter type telly programme. When the story kicks off, she's on her final assignment. She's spending the night in a hotel in an unnamed and small South American country before heading out to interview a scientist involved in conservation, which is the subject of the whole assignment. Frankly, she's not enjoying the experience. It's hot, room service is rotten and the air conditioning's on the blink. She thinks things can't get any worse. But then there's a knock at the door. It's not a bloke here to fix the air conditioning, it's her cameraman, Dave McCormick, who also happens to be her ex-boyfriend. The split is recent and still hurts both of them, though they both hide it. She uses sarcasm, he feigns indifference. The inference is that Dave was carrying on with the programme's producer, Maria. (Who takes a terrible slagging all through, incidentally).

At the research complex Katya and Dave will be visiting (along with the sound-man and director if they ever get through customs – which they don't), things are not all sweetness and light. Dr Imogen Petersen is talking with a Captain Sanchez of the local army. She's worried about security in the compound – 4 of her colleagues were killed by guerrillas recently and there was a huge explosion in the jungle nearby a few days before. Sanchez is more worried that Petersen will blab to the TV people about guerrillas and terrorists, which would not be good for tourism or the country's international image. It's also clear that Petersen has absolutely nothing to do with conservation. That is certainly part of what goes on here in the compound, but she is working on something totally different. Something extraordinary. A medical discovery so profound it will make penicillin look like the stone age. She's eyeing a Nobel Prize, a place in history and a whopping great stack of cash at the end of this. Eventually she agrees to act like a nice little scientist when the TV people are here. There's a degree of disdain going both ways between Petersen and Sanchez. They may have a certain respect for each other professionally, but personally they're not bosom buddies. Sanchez heads off out into the compound to check on security – and to get away from the scientist. He sees a soldier he doesn't recognise and chases the soldier. He thinks he sees the man run into Doctor Muller's research tent – except Muller's the only one there and he didn't see anybody else. (Muller, incidentally, is the scientist in charge of the conservation work). Sanchez is worried.

If a guerrilla has sneaked into the compound, they could be in big trouble.

Dave and Kat are being driven to the compound on the bumpiest, rockiest road ever built. Dave has tried to get a conversation going with Kat but she's giving him the silent treatment. After considerable goading he finally manages to push Kat into telling him to shut up. It's not great conversation but it's a start. And then he spots something out of the window. Kat thinks he's just trying to keep the conversation going. He's not. This is serious. A few seconds later bullets slam into the 4by4 they're riding in. They flatten themselves and their driver drives as fast as he can. Dave seems more worried about his camera than his health. Kat pulls him back down out of sight of the guerrillas until they've rounded a bend and are out of sight. Kat suffers the indignity of getting a bit of glass in the bum. Which Dave tries hard not to find funny. But fails.

At the compound, Sanchez is not a happy captain. No sign of the mystery soldier. He orders that the perimeter fence be examined again, and that the dogs be prepared for patrol duty in the compound at night. Petersen's a bit worried by this, especially with the TV people arriving. On cue, the bullet-ridden 4by4 chunters into the compound. Sanchez greets them. He's appalled by them having been attacked but blames it on a battle from a neighbouring country spilling over the border. Petersen tends to Kat's wounded pride (and bum) while Sanchez gets what info about the guerrillas he can from Dave. Here we get an inkling that Dave knows a sight more about military ops than a cameraman on a Blue Peter type show should. He knows makes of guns, calibre of weapon... that sort of thing. Sanchez clocks this as well, in an understated way. Sanchez heads outside and collars a soldier. There's still no sign of the mystery soldier, and the patrols have turned up a blank on the guerrillas – "Hardly surprising," grumbles Sanchez. "They were too busy shooting at the British TV people to wait around for you to find them. Where are they? Where are they and what kind of artillery do they have that could cause the explosion from a few nights before? He's worried.

Out on the jungle, Marina Silvestra, leader of the guerrillas isn't going to win any smiley-face contests either. She's raging that her troops attacked the 4by4. Don't they understand that if their organisation is ever to be seen as more than a terrorist outfit, they have to win the hearts and minds of the people, not only of

their own country but of the world as well. Shooting a kids' TV
personality, however understandable (at least in Andi Peters' case
if you ask me, not that you did) is not going to make them seem
like a credible political force. She's also a bit worried that one of
her soldiers and someone from the compund have been found
dead. Not just dead, either. Horrible markings on them shwing
that they died in pain. A warning to Marina and her troops that
they will be horribly executed if they don't clear off. Marina's not
for clearing off. And she's more than capable of matching
whatever brutality is thrown at her. She's been fighting all her
life. She's fought her way out of the gutter, off the streets, away
from the perverts and pimps who tried to use and abuse her, she's
fought to be more than a nothing. She's fought hard to educate
herself. Now she's fighting so that other people won't have to go
through the childhood she had. Crossing this woman would be
dangerous. She is intelligent, articulate and deadly. She doesn't
consider herself a terrorist or a guerrilla – she is a soldier. She
knows something's more important than conservation is going on
in the compound. And she wants an enemy soldier captured to
find out what's going on. She wants to know why her men were
brutalised.

In the compound, Kat and Dave can see the high level of
security. They are still not on the best of terms. The majority of
their conversations consist of sniping and bitching but they both
have the idea that there's more going on here than just
conservation. They decide to have a shufti at the sort of tent/hut
thing Petersen works in. They've been seeing slightly odd
shenanigans at this tent. It's got heavier security than any of the
others – a more complex number pad "43046721" says Dave.
"Eight number combination." He's been paying attention. And
it's another hint that there's more than meets the eye to Dave. For
the most part, he's relaxed, indifferent. Sometimes, though, there
are flashes of him being altogether more tuned in. Kat is quite
unsettled by this side of him. They were together for almost two
years and she never saw this aspect of his personality. He is at
ease creeping about the compound, avoiding sentries and timing
their movements against the sweeps of the surveillance cameras.
They have almost made it to the tent/hut they are heading for
when they see a soldier moving towards it. And he's acting
suspiciously as well. Dave starts filming the soldier. The soldier
doesn't know the combination – so he shouldn't be going in there

obviously. He produces a weird, torch-like device and points it at the lock, which fritzes and crackles and then clocks open. The soldier is about to go in when there's an explosion nearby. He is thrown off his feet by the blast. The compound is immediately full of troops and scientists. Sneaking into the hut is a non-starter. The shady soldier is still down on the ground and Kat goes to help him, but he pushes her aside and runs. Sanchez arrives. He sees the camera, the open hut and the compound under attack. Kat and Dave are, in all but name, arrested and taken to his office for questioning.

In the jungles surrounding the compound, Marina is slightly happier now that she has struck back. Word comes to her that a soldier was seen hurrying out of the compound into the jungle. A deserter? A coward? Easier to interrogate than a brave soldier. She wants the runaway soldier found and brought to her. He doesn't have to be in perfect health either.

Dave and Kat are being interrogated by Sanchez. He has had them checked out. Kat is a reporter who stumbled into presenting kids' TV by being fun, photogenic and looking for a job. Her real name is Kathy Delaney but she changed it for telly. He's not overly worried by her. Dave, on the other hand, is an altogether different kettle of fish. Dave has a history as a war cameraman. He was behind the lines with the SAS during the Gulf War, worked in Northern Ireland, went undercover in Tennessee with the KKK, and more recently (1998/99-ish – a few years earlier) was in Afghanistan covering human rights violations by the government of the time. And now he's... a children's TV cameraman? Sanchez seems to be jumping to the obvious conclusion that Dave's here to look for a bigger story than a bit of fluffy time-filling for kids at tea-time. Dave protests that he is what he seems to be. He used to be a war cameraman, now he does kids TV. Why the change? She's sitting next to him. Kat had asked him to stop taking the dangerous assignments and he had agreed. Sanchez isn't buying the story, but Kat backs it up. But it's the first time she's heard about some of the stories Dave had covered. He never mentioned some of them – particularly the one with the SAS. Sanchez picks up on that and drops in an interesting tit-bit – the rumour that Dave had been given special privileges by the SAS after killing an enemy soldier to save a member of the SAS. Dave won't confirm or deny that he killed anybody, saying only that it was a long time ago. Kat is now sure that she knows even less about him than she thought.

The soldier who ran from the camp has been caught and knocked unconscious. He is delivered to Marina, who is less than gentle in her interrogation. The soldier seems to fall unconscious again after a few minor thumps. He's been unresponsive, refusing to answer any questions. Marina wonders if he's a good soldier or just plain stupid. She leaves him to stew. She tells her soldiers not to be overly gentle with their guest.

In the scientific compound, Dave and Kat are, in all but name, prisoners. For their own good, naturally, according to Sanchez. They're locked up together and Kat is wary of Dave. She's wondering if he really is a killer. Could she have lived for the best part of two years with someone who had deliberately killed another human being? Dave, on the other hand, is wondering about how to get out. It's clear that there's a damn sight more happening here than conservation. What's in the hut everybody wants to get inside? Who are the guerrillas? What's their objective? He's sure they won't find any answers as long as they're stuck inside. They're going to have to escape.

Sanchez is getting worried. Two of his patrols haven't come back and another reported in as being under attack before being cut off. He asks how far along Imogen's research is. Is it far enough along for them to be able to move it back to a city, where they'll be safe? Imogen's not sure. Some of the experiments could be transplanted but the Wo Jifo flower is very delicate. It doesn't travel well. It would have to be airlifted out. That suits Sanchez. Things are starting to go very wrong here and he doesn't want more dead scientists on his record. He's eyeing a place in the government eventually – an ambitious sort. He decides to call for an airlift.

Marina listens in to the request for an airlift, eavesdropping on a radio. This suits her. A helicopter is a much bigger target to shoot at than a person. When she goes back to the interrogation, both the soldier and his guard are gone. There are signs of a struggle. This has made her mind up for her. If the soldier gets back to the compound, her camp will be under immediate attack. The best option left to her is to attack. Attack the compound and attack the helicopter.

Imogen is discussing the implications of moving back to the city with Muller. He really is a conservationist. He knows that his research here was never the prime concern but it matters to him and he doesn't want to go back, his job half done. Imogen couldn't give a toss if Muller goes back to the city or not but Sanchez has his career to think about so everybody's going to be safe, whether they like it or not.

Kat and Dave have escaped from their makeshift cell. Now they see Sanchez entering the mystery tent/hut. They follow him in – and find Sanchez searching the place. Very suspicious. Why is he looking for something? And what's the something in question? And an equally pertinent question arrives when the hut door opens and who arrives? Sanchez. There are two Captain Sanchezes. Which causes some confusion. (And will have to be carefully handled otherwise the listeners will become just as confused). Imogen enters and she hasn't a clue which Sanchez is which either. The Sanchezes are wary of each other. And then they attack each other. The other people in the room have no idea what to do – how can they begin to explain two Sanchezes? One pulls a gun and tries to shoot the other one – he only manages to wing him. He barges past the other Sanchez and runs off into the night, leaving the other Sanchez with a slightly bloodied head and three shocked people who don't know if he's the real deal or not. And Sanchez is interested to know what Dave and Kat were doing snooping around an off-limits area when they should have been safely locked up like good little prisoners.

And then the attack comes. The guerrillas hit the base hard. Dave and Kat try to get some answers but there's chaos all around them. And then Kat spots something about the blood from the wound (Dave thinks it's a hell of a time for her to get gory) but he and then Imogen agree that something's not right with the blood. The colour is just a bit off, it's thinner than usual blood and it's not congealing properly. She looks at it under the microscope – it's not blood as she knows it. If she didn't know better she'd say that it wasn't human blood.

The battle isn't going well. The guerrillas are over-running the compound – the helicopter is shot down as it gets closer. In the middle of the battle, Marina corners Sanchez. She has a good old gloat and is about to kill him when she sees that he's already nursing an injury. From his own people, no doubt. Sanchez replies that his own people have injured themselves for too long. He gets a bit odd on the subject and then just gets very odd indeed. He changes shape in front of Marina – to a Zygon. She's freaked out and then sees the other Sanchez – just in time to be captured, as is the Zygon, which is pretty much turfed into a cage.

The guerrillas' attack is repelled and Marina is now captured. Sanchez is seeing something spectacular in front of himself. If he brings in this alien and the terrorist leader he'll be El Presedente quicker than a hiccup. He thinks the alien is working with Marina. She accuses the government of being involved. Dave and Kat are being kept out of it until Sanchez decides that he needs a record of his great triumph. This would put him right up there with all the great leaders of the world. He quite fancies that idea. Kat is told that she'll be doing the spiel to camera – and that she'd better make Sanchez sound good.

Dave and Kat reluctantly agree to go through with this, given that the alternative would seem to be an accidental but quick death. They are tense and on edge and bicker about their failed relationship. She accuses him regarding his affair with their boss. Which, he finally denies. The first time he's ever just come straight out and said there was no fling. She doesn't believe him. Why didn't he just say so earlier? And what has he been spending so much time with the afore-insulted Maria? You should get the feeling that this is the first time they've actually talked about any of this. They're both stubborn and strong-willed – and very proud. Neither will entertain the possibility that they could have been wrong. As for the story... well, Dave is a cameraman and Kat has always dreamed of reporting as Katherine Dylan, BBC Ten O'Clock news. Maybe this is her chance.

Imogen is fascinated by the captive alien, although Sanchez refuses to let her tend to the Zygon's wound. Muller is also fascinated by the alien. He's been staying out of the way, doing the most sensible thing possible during the battle – keeping his head down and trying to avoid getting shot.

Sanchez has been interrogating both Marina and the Zygon – both of whom show utter disdain for him, and for each other, despite the Zygon's protests that it didn't kill Marina's men in the jungle. It doesn't give a toss that the men are dead, but does want it known that he didn't kill them.

Imogen looks in to check on the two prisoners. Whether Sanchez likes it or not, she's going to make sure they're okay (mainly the Zygon – Marina can pretty much go to hell as far as Imogen's concerned). Marina is asleep or more likely unconscious. The Zygon may well be playing possum but it's an incredible scientific opportunity she's not prepared to miss out on. Muller arrives and warns Imogen to steer clear of the alien. Sanchez won't like her ignoring his orders – and the alien has already shown itself to be dangerous. They are disagreeing when Sanchez arrives. He's not happy that they're with his captives but he's more interested in making his play for power. He's preparing to speak to camera when Marina is wakened. She refuses to speak and then sees Muller – and freaks out (technical medical term). She goes mental. She's seen this guy – and he was dead at the time. Sanchez wallops her and tells her to shut up. But she's insistent. She saw the other one change shape – and it's Dave who goes to the top of the class by piecing together that if the alien is a shape-changer, then maybe this isn't Muller at all. It's another shape-changer. Sanchez pretty much thinks this is nuts, but the already-captured Zygon starts going loopy, trying to get away from Muller. Kat pitches in. How about an easy test. Imogen said that Zygon blood was nothing like human blood. A sample from Muller would do the trick. Sanchez still thinks this is a load of old cobblers – until Muller refuses. He attacks Sanchez and escapes, also attacking Marina as he goes.

It's clear that the Muller Zygon isn't working with Marina. A truce is called – albeit an uneasy one. The Zygon has to be caught. Marina's few guerrillas are sent out with troops (to use the guerrillas' knowledge of the jungle) in a search for the Zygon.

In the compound, Kat is troubled by something. If Muller's also a Zygon, why was the captive Zygon so afraid of it? She tries talking to the beast. It's not overly responsive but she and Imogen eventually get it talking. The creature in the shape of Muller is indeed another Zygon – but one with a different view of life. A different perspective on the plight of the Zygon race, with regards to their lack of a home planet. Most Zygons favour nicking a planet and slowly altering it suit their race's needs. But this is a long-term plan and the Zygons don't have the forces to actively conquer a world. The captive Zygon has a different plan – to alter the Zygons themselves to suit the planet they're on. To do that, it would need a particular drug – which just happens to be the Wo Jifo flower that Imogen's been working with. The drug she's been working on will allow the Zygons to deal more easily with other atmospheres – it'll allow them a degree of enforced evolution, which is an abhorrent, immoral and entirely unacceptable idea to the other side of the argument. One thing is clear, though. Both factions of the Zygon schism (which is serious inside the Zygon social system) want to take Earth for themselves. Neither is overly keen on sharing Earth with the hairy monkeys who wander about ruining the planet, thinking they own the place and think they are unable to function unless they have a mobile phone. (Nothing to do with the plot but I hate mobile phones, especially when you're on the train.) Both factions of Zygons would look to take humans out of the equation, which rules out helping one side against the other.

Out in the jungle, Marina and Sanchez aren't getting along either. Even though they're supposed to be working together, it's clear that they'd rather tear each other apart. In the jungle, they find a spaceship. They enter and look around. It's a weird kind of ship. They don't see any kind of technology they can snaffle – but on the bright side, there don't seem to be any other Zygons either. Until one slips out, leaving the ship alarmingly active. It's going to blow up.

At the compound, a huge explosion is heard. Sanchez returns, much the worse for wear. The ship exploded and Marina was killed. They have to get the Zygon creature away from the compound. They are getting ready to move the Zygon when Marina arrives. She's in a bad way as well. But she claims that Sanchez is dead and that this must be a Zygon copy. Sanchez claims that Marina is the fake.

The compound shakes – something is overhead. The captive Zygon tries to escape. It has to be the other Zygon's spaceship. Coming to rescue the captive Zygon says Sanchez. Or coming to destroy the compound, suggests Kat. Dave's trying to weigh it all out. He suggests waiting – if they run, the ship may well attack them. If they wait, there's the chance that they won't be attacked because they have at least one alien with them and the Zygons probably wouldn't want to kill their own kind. Marina's against this. Sanchez thinks it would give them time to work out a plan. They argue again. Dave and Kat quietly discuss the fact that either Sanchez or Marina is a Zygon and they don't know which. On the other hand, somebody in the room might be able to tell who it is. They release the captive Zygon, who attacks Sanchez. Sanchez reverts to Zygon form and the two battle their way out into the compound. The humans now can't tell which Zygon is which – not that it matter since they're both intent on taking Earth one way or the other. The Zygon ship is hovering overhead, observing the battle below.

Imogen wants to go to the lab to save her work on the Wo Jifo, which sets minds working. What else does she have in the lab? Marina is convinced that the Zygon technology is organic – and if the Wo Jifo can help the Zygons, Imogen must have something in the lab that's lethal to organic life – or at least harmful to it, if only for experimentation purposes. She does. That would look to be their best bet of getting rid of the ship.

Before setting off, Dave owns up to Kat why he spent so much time with bitch-boss Maria – he was arranging a move for himself from kids TV back to the news. Partly because he wanted to get into the production side, but mainly because (although she hasn't heard yet) when she gets back, Kat is going to be offered a slot with the news – albeit very junior and lowly. At best she'll be 3rd reserve for Jenny Bond and will spend her first year doing the cheery segments that turn up at the end of broadcasts. Budgies that know the words to Rule Britannia, skateboarding grannies, grocers shops that sell vegetables which look remarkably like celebrities – the "and finally" slot. But it's a start. That's what he's been up to. He has not been playing away with Maria. Why didn't he just say that? Because he's stubborn and pig-headed and he was angry that Kat had jumped to conclusions. And he wasn't particularly in the mood to defend himself against stupid accusations she should have known better than make. But as she rightly points out, if he had been more open there wouldn't have been any need for accusations. They agree to talk this out later.

Dave and Imogen make the run to the lab. They get the toxic material, which is stored in flasks, at below zero temperatures. All they have to do now is get it up to the spaceship. How? How should Dave know? He's making it up on the hoof.

One of the Zygons kills the other and goes into the lab. It demands the Wo Jifo extract, which Dave hands over only when Imogen is threatened. The Zygon enters the ship, which takes off again. Marina has been injured again by the Zygon and Kat has a clean shot at it, but Dave stops her from shooting. His then the suggestion is that the survivors run like hell. The Zygon ship is looking unsteady. It wobbles (so we're told in non-clunky expository dialogue) and then starts to fall from the sky. It lands in the compound, just giving the humans time to get clear. There's an explosion and fire from the crash. The fire will destroy the dangerous chemicals – but it has ruined the work Imogen did on the Wo Jifo as well. She decides to stay in the jungle and try again, even though there'll be no backing. She's not doing it for humanity – she still wants the glory and eventually, the cash. Marina will help – because it'll show her guerrillas in a good light.

Kat and Dave head back to the city on horseback – the only transport available. They're still bickering, but are on better terms now. His camera's been destroyed – by Marina to stop more people coming into the jungle. Kat mutters that nobody would believe them anyway. Dave lobs something to her – a tape. He took it from the camera before it was destroyed. He's spent too much time behind enemy lines to get caught out that easily. It's her first scoop. As for their relationship? Well, they'll see, although they'll probably be bickering over whether or not they'll see.

Main characters

Kat
Dave
Captain Sanchez
Imogen
Muller
Marina Silvestra

Notes

This was one of the two story outlines I sent to BBV after *The Eye of the Scorpion* came out. It went in at the same time as *Time Heals All Things*. This was the one that they showed interest in taking forward. I swapped some emails with David Elms and Bill Baggs at BBV about what we'd do with the story. I was due to sit down with Bill Baggs at the Gallifrey One convention in Los Angeles and discuss it with him there. However, my uncle died and I had to cancel out on going to the convention. I emailed BBV a few times after that but there was no word back on the story going forward. I moved on with other projects and just accepted that it was had gone to the great place in the sky where dead stories go. I haven't really looked at it since. Normally I keep all my old stories logged in the back of my head. I can often pluck bits and pieces from unused and abandoned stories to drop into a new project. If that sounds like cheating, it's not. If you've worked on something and you can use it in a different story than you originally thought... do it. If it's good it's worth using. I cannibalise my own ideas regularly. That all comes from one of the best bits of advice I was ever given – never throw anything away. Think of it as like cooking. If you buy ingredients for a recipe but decide not to make the dish, you don't just throw away the ingredients. You use them in a different recipe. Writing is exactly the same. Hang onto your ideas, recycle what you haven't been able to use elsewhere. It's your work, you've put time, sweat and effort into it, so don't waste it. I have folder if ideas on my desktop and a stack of notebooks beside the desk filled with all the notes made for stories from around 2000 onwards.

Kill or Cure has some interesting things in it. Unfortunately, the most interesting thing isn't mine – it's the Zygons. They are one of *Doctor Who*'s most interesting and, until the 50th anniversary, underused monsters.. They're a fabulous creation. Early in 2015, Thebes Publishing tried to get the licence to publish a Zygon novel. I wasn't going to write it. I was Editor-in-Chief and I had a respected thriller writer in mind for the job. We approached Robert Banks Stewart through his agent but we didn't get anywhere. I don't know why. Whether it was part of his deal for the BBC using the Zygons or if he simply didn't think the deal we offered was of a level that he considered agreeable, we don't

know. Whatever the reason, it was entirely within Robert Banks'
Stewart rights to decline the offer. It's a pity, but he create the
Zygons and what he did with the rights was entirely up to him. He
and his agent were courteous and professional all the way
through, so I have no complaints.

I do like the idea of a schism in Zygon society. I'm intrigued
by civil wars. Apart from 'civil war' being an oxymoron. I'm
intrigued by the forces that would force a nation, species, planet,
religion or any kind of society into splitting. At what point does
the thing that brought them together break so badly that it splits
them apart? And what can be so bad that it splits them? I wrote
about the American Civil War in *Blood and Hope*, the *Doctor
Who* novella I did for Telos Publishing. I did a lot of research for
that book, and that was probably what took me from interested in
the subject to fascinated by it. *Blood and Hope* was published in
2004, but I wrote the first draft in 2002, so I wrote *Kill or Cure*
when I still had my civil war research fresh in my mind. How
would an alien civilisation deal with a civil war or a dissenter? It
was a notion I held onto for another later pitch with a different
monster (and a very different story) but I'll save discussing that
for another time.

I had some concerns about stereotyping in this story when I
was working it out. I didn't want Kat to be an airhead bimbo. I
wanted her to be someone with serious ambitions who was trying
to work her way from children's TV up to being a serious TV
news journalist. She's ambitious and she's intelligent and she's
feeling strangled by having to call everything 'awesome' and
'fantastic'. The real question I had, though, was in how the South
American characters would be portrayed. Hollywood has a bad
history of treating Latin characters as shifty, untrustworthy and
highly strung. Setting the story in South America, I was conscious
of that. There's no reason why I would have fallen into that cliché
but it never hurts to remind yourself of things to avoid. Real
people with real reactions and real emotions are far more
interesting than clichés. Even if you're writing science fiction or
fantasy, if you can keep the characters and emotions real you
have a better chance of drawing your audience into the story.
Maintaining 'reality' in the story doesn't mean you have to go for
scientific accuracy. The important thing is to maintain the
integrity of the universe you're building. If you say gravity on a
world is twenty percent of that on Earth, then you have to follow

through on gravity being twenty percent on that planet all the way through your story. So, if somebody jumps, you have to take that lower gravity into account. If something is thrown, you have to remember that twenty percent gravity. It's the same with characterisation. If you say that the military run a nation, you don't then have politicians appear in charge. You maintain the integrity of the world and you build and embellish it. Take the situation you've created, stay true to it and grow your universe. Give it detail and background. Personally, I prefer to do that a bit at a time, throwing in little details regularly so that the audience can pick on them and immerse themselves fully in that world. I learned pretty early to avoid just giving an avalanche of information. An infodump is inelegant, it sounds clunky and amateur and it will make you wince when you look back at it.

Available now from
THEBES PUBLISHING

KERIDES THE THINKER
The Collected Scripts, Volume One

Egypt, 276BC

Kerides, a penniless young Greek student arrives in Egypt's capital city, Alexandria, seeking to pursue his studies. With the help, occasional hindrance and regular insults of former slave, Adrea, Kerides finds that murders and mysteries have a regular habit of interrupting his studies.

Together, they face merciless assassins, brutal ancient cults, betrayal, an attack on Egypt itself and a marketplace fortune teller claiming to be the reincarnation of an uncrowned pharaoh… and the strange thing is, she seems to be telling the truth. They even manage to find time for a trip to the fabled Library of Alexandria, only to find that the librarian had been checked out for good.

These scripts are episodes 1-8 of the popular Imagination Theater radio series, *Kerides The Thinker*, and each script is accompanied by notes by the writers.

The double-length Episode 8, *Return of the Queen*, features the uncrowned Pharaoh Erimem, from the universe of **Doctor Who**.

Volume Two also available.

Available now from
THEBES PUBLISHING

THE HEART OF FRANKENSTEIN
and other Collected Radio Horror Scripts

"What am I? Am I God's creature or Victor Frankenstein's?"

Shocked and tormented by the sudden accidental death of his beautiful wife, Baron Victor Frankenstein challenges death and God in a desperate attempt to bring his wife back from the grave.

But brutal killings soon follow Elizabeth's rebirth. Is the woman who came back to him the same person she was before or has Victor Frankenstein created a monster?

Also featured in the collection:

CURSE OF THE MUMMY
"I am a living god. I do not apologise. My word is law, my thoughts are the forces that shape the world. I cannot make mistakes. I cannot be wrong. I cannot be defied."

MAESTRO: THE DEMON OF SACRE MERE
"Leonardo, nobody has heard of this village because, despite the fact that we are here, it does not seem to exist."

THE FURTHER ADVENTURES OF SHERLOCK HOLMES: THE CURSED OF BROKENSHORE
"I fear, Mr Holmes, that the dead are walking in Brokenshore."

Baron Frankenstein, Leonardo daVinci, Sherlock Holmes and the Mummy in four spine-chilling scripts originally written for radio.

MOVIE STAR

A WOMAN MURDERED. A DREAM KILLED.

*Everybody comes to Hollywood... not
everybody survives.*

**Detective Jim Munro just pulled a case that
could make a career.**
Or kill it.
**A woman found murdered in LA. Her name was
Chelsea Raines, she was a porn star and she
was mutilated, cut to pieces while she was
still alive.**
**Investigating Chelsea's broken dream of
Hollywood fame leads Munro to the world of
the porn industry, to brutal murder and to his
only solid lead, a model named Alexa.**
**Pressured by his superiors and city politics,
the investigation could kill more than just
Munro's career.**

Available now from
THEBES PUBLISHING

ERIMEM

THE LAST PHARAOH

by Iain McLaughlin and Claire Bartlett
Foreword by Caroline Morris

After a freak electrical storm that seems to happen indoors, a young woman is found in the Egyptian exhibit of a London museum, and she seems to look exactly like the face on the death-mask of the uncrowned Pharaoh Erimem…

What is she doing inside the exhibit? How did she get there? Is she really a Pharaoh from 1400BC? And just who is willing to search time and space to find and assassinate her?

THE LAST PHARAOH is the first in a series of novels, novellas and short story anthologies taking Erimem, a former companion of the 5th Doctor, on a new set of adventures travelling to the past, the future and into deep space.

THE LAST PHARAOH takes Erimem and a group of 21st century students far into the past, to Actium in Greece where Erimem meets the famed Cleopatra VII on the eve of a vital battle which could end Egypt's existence as a free country and condemn it to life as a Roman province. Two great rulers of Egypt come into conflict over what Egypt needs to do in order to survive, and both Erimem and Cleopatra face their own personal battles for survival.

ERIMEM

ALREADY AVAILABLE

THE BEAST OF STALINGRAD
A novella by Iain McLaughlin

INTO THE UNKNOWN
A collection of short stories

PRIME IMPERATIVE
A novella by Julianne Todd

COMING SOON

A PHARAOH OF MARS
A novel by Jim Mortimore

BUCCANEER
A novella by Iain McLaughlin

THREE FACES OF HELENA
A collection of three novellas

www.ingramcontent.com/pod-product-compliance
Lightning Source LLC
Chambersburg PA
CBHW070020100426
42740CB00013B/2565